CAVENDISH

CAVENDISH

Its People and Its Heritage

Edited by

Rosemary Freeth

Published by

The Cavendish Book Project 2002

This publication was made possible through the financial support of the
Local Heritage Initiative and Cavendish Parish Council

ISBN No 0 9542219 0 7

Cover photograph by Philip Aspinall

Printed in Great Britain at
The Lavenham Press Limited, Lavenham, Suffolk

Contents

Foreword	vii
Preface	ix
Acknowledgements	xi
Introduction	1
Earliest Times	3
The Manors	7
Families	15
Charities and Trusts	26
Agriculture	31
The Weather	42
Flora and Fauna	46
Buildings through the Village	63
Schooling – Then and Now	82
Churches	96
Public Services	106
Transport	116
Trade and Industry	124
Organisations and Activities	140
Postscript	161
Bibliography	163
Index	165

Foreword

by

His Grace the Duke of Devonshire

Chatsworth
Bakewell
Derbyshire
DE45 1PP

I was very pleased to be asked to write a foreword for this book.

Our family name is derived from Cavendish and we have had links here for generations.

I have very fond memories of visits to the village myself and I have always found the people of Cavendish to be warm and friendly with a great pride in their heritage.

I hope that you will enjoy this account of their lovely village.

Foreword by His Grace the Duke of Devonshire

Preface

Three projects were undertaken in Cavendish as a way of celebrating the millennium. Michael Pizzey arranged for photographs to be taken of residents and their houses as a record for the village at a point in time. A video was produced by Dick Comyn about the village including contributions from long time Cavendish residents. I co-ordinated the third project which was the production of an illustrated parish map by a team of people recruited from across the community.

It was during the work on the map that I became aware of the wealth of information about the village which could be recorded given further time and space. Thus the idea of the book was born.

I applied for a grant from the Local Heritage Initiative, which is a partnership between the Heritage Lottery Fund, the Nationwide Building Society and the Countryside Agency. The application was successful and I was fortunate to receive some additional financial support from Cavendish Parish Council.

The project was organised so as to involve the community with regular meetings of a core group of village residents who undertook research and made contact with many people and organisations both in and outside Cavendish. All age groups have contributed and those people who live in some of the older buildings were asked to provide background details. The amount of information which has been unearthed across the village could have filled many volumes but the limitations on the book size have meant that not all the interesting facts and photographs could be included.

The book has been written not as a history since there are many better qualified to do so, but as an account of many aspects of village life both past and present.

It is hoped that the book will provide a worthwhile record of Cavendish for residents and visitors alike both now and in the future.

Rosemary Freeth

Acknowledgements

We are grateful to the many people in Cavendish who have loaned documents or fielded endless questions about aspects of village life as they remember it. We thank them for their interest and encouragement. We also thank Fred Pawsey and the late Patrick O'Connell for some pages of text.

We are also appreciative of the contributions from people and organisations outside the village particularly His Grace, The Duke of Devonshire, Olive Bettinson, Colin and Barbara Brown, Rodney Bullock, Chris Copp, Ellen Corner, Margaret Ebeling, Mark Ebeling, Gladys Farrington, Sir Patrick Gillam, Ron Hartley, Tom Hastie, Mary Jackson, James Jones, Paul Martindill, Nick Mason, Ted Ritchie, Angela Steed, Clive Stewart, Alfred Tharby, Mike Vincent, EMI Records, Otley College, Suffolk Archaeological Services, Suffolk Libraries, Suffolk Records Office and Suffolk Wildlife Trust.

Our special thanks to Anne Heffernan and Judy Kemp for their illustrations.

We are also indebted to the following for the loan of old pictures:- Basil Ambrose, Betty Armon-Jones, Margaret Ebeling, Jeremy Eldridge, Maurice Finbow, Dorothy Jackson, Peggy Jackson, Brian Kemp, Pam Nevard, Barbara Parr, David Playle, Ernie Playle, Frances Simmons, Edith Skeemer, Sallie Starie, Ruth Steed, Margaret Swithinbank, Mrs Taylor, Fred Turkentine, Mary Turkentine and John Wayman.

In writing a book such as this it is impossible to include all the information supplied. We have endeavoured to verify facts where possible but apologise in advance for any omissions or errors.

Members of the Cavendish Book Project

Rosemary Freeth, Denise Davies, Brenda Grimmett, Dorothy Jackson, Peggy Jackson, Frances Simmons, Ruth Steed

Aerial View of Cavendish from Lower Street — *Pete Walton*

INTRODUCTION

Cavendish is an attractive village situated along the Stour Valley between Long Melford and Clare in Suffolk. The parish covers some 3354 acres and much of it is given over to arable farming. The River Stour acts as the county boundary to the south, and it is here in the valley that the soil is mainly light sandy loam ranging to heavy clay loam on higher ground. A triangulation pillar well north of Colts Hall marks the highest point in the village and the second highest point in Suffolk at 342 feet (104m).

The population was recorded as 33 in 1086 and peaked at 1394 in 1851. The 19th century trade directories show, from the shops and businesses listed, how self sufficient Cavendish was at that time. The latest figures from Suffolk County Council give a population of 970 and this number will be ratified when the 2001 census details are made available.

Cavendish is famous for its picturesque green and cottages. Cavendish is also the family name of the Dukes of Devonshire who are descended from a William Cavendish who sold the manor in 1569.

There are in fact four other places in the world which bear the name of Cavendish – in Alberta, Canada; Vermont, USA; Prince Edward Island, Canada; and in Victoria, Australia. Cavendish in Vermont was for a time home to the exiled Russian writer Solzhenitsyn; Cavendish on Prince Edward Island was the setting for L M Montgomery's series of books about Anne of Green Gables; and cricketers from Cavendish in Australia have been over to play against the village team in Suffolk.

There is however more to Cavendish, Suffolk than the famous view on greetings cards, chocolate boxes, calendars, jigsaws and even grass seed packets! It is hoped that in these pages some of the features which make Cavendish special will be found.

Photograph of the items found in Michael Pizzey's garden. 1. Belemnite 2. Ammonite 3. Flake tool 4. Fossilised mud 5. Gryphaea   *Andrew Norman*

EARLIEST TIMES

Early life and habitation

Evidence of early life in its many forms can be found in fossils and other artefacts unearthed in the village. When gardening it is often the case that 'things of interest' have been found with the intention of learning about them at a later date. Michael Pizzey has done just that. Over the years he has dug up various interesting looking objects and put them to one side. He recently took them to the Sedgwick Museum of Geology in Cambridge so that they could be examined and dated.

It appears that when the first houses in Peacocks Close were being built the subsoil was dug out and dumped towards the top of the site where it was left without a covering of topsoil. This soil formed the gardens of the houses at that end of the development and it is in this earth that Michael has made his discoveries.

The earliest item found was a lump of fossilised mud with ironstone casing clearly showing. This was dated by the museum to about 200 million years old.

Some of the fossils which were discovered demonstrate the type of creatures living at the time – about 150 million years ago. They include belemnites which were a type of marine animal whose closest living relatives are squid and cuttlefish; a rusty ammonite which is a type of mollusc; and a gryphaea. The latter is also known as a 'devil's toenail' and was a type of bivalve mollusc. The illustration shows the muscle scar where the animal was attached to the shell. These fossils are from the Jurassic period but Michael has found no evidence of a dinosaur - yet!

Another find of significance was that of a flake tool made of flint during the Palaeolithic or Old Stone Age period about (150 – 200,000 years ago) and seems to show that early man was living in the area then and making flint tools.

Evidence of later habitation somewhere in the valley is indicated by ring-ditches which are all that remain of probable Bronze Age round barrows or burial mounds. These were flattened long ago and are no longer visible to the casual observer and only very occasionally to experts flying high above them when the season and ground conditions are right. It is not known where or how many early people may have lived here at this time (2700 – 1500 BC), but the river and its valley must have been an attraction for growing crops and rearing animals.

It is likely that parts of the valley had settlements during the Iron Age. Many years ago an Iron Age pot was found in the River Stour. At this time the tribe living in the southern half of Suffolk were the Trinovantes with the Iceni occupying the northern part.

The First Millennium

By the start of the first millennium it is possible to link the place now known as Cavendish with events occurring across a wider region.

In 1 AD Cavendish was in that part of Europe which the Romans knew as 'Britain' and stretching from Land's End to John O'Groats. It was a land of many tribes. In this area our tribe was the Trinovantes whose lands included the southern half of Suffolk, Essex to the River Thames as well as parts of Hertfordshire and Cambridgeshire.

By 43 AD Britain had become a target for incorporation into the Roman Empire. When Claudius became emperor the order to invade was given and a large force of 40,000 legionnaires set sail from Boulogne for the Kent coast. They landed near Richborough and, after a battle for the Medway crossing, moved northwards until they reached the Thames and Westminster. They awaited the arrival of Emperor Claudius to take charge of military operations. In the ensuing battle with the Roman legions, one of the kings of the Trinovantes was killed. Caractacus, the other king, managed to escape. The war continued under the leadership of Caractacus until he was captured five years later. Prior to the execution he was paraded in chains but due to his brave and noble demeanour he was pardoned by Claudius.

Less compassion was shown to Queen Boudicca of the Iceni, the neighbouring tribe in Norfolk. In 60 AD she and her daughters suffered cruelly at the hands of Roman soldiers. Whilst the Roman Governor, Suetonius Paulinus and his elite legions were battling with the rebellious druids of Anglesea she took her revenge. She attacked Colchester, then St Albans and finally London and burned them to the ground together with their inhabitants. On return to Colchester the Roman Governor took action, executed the leaders of the rebellion and tortured or enslaved many of their followers.

The governor, Suetonius Paulinus, was soon dismissed. The procurator, Julius, had sent a damning report on his handling of the Trinovantes and Iceni. The taxes and exports of this region had brought in good returns to the Roman treasury and the killing or torture of the farmers and labourers had put these incomes at risk.

For a period after the conquest, Britain was at peace. Throughout East Anglia Roman law and order prevailed and the new masters began to turn southern Britain into a 'Colonia' or Roman province. Tribal kings and queens continued to exercise authority but subject to the wishes of successive Roman governors.

Trade was important in Suffolk both internally and for export to the continent. Then, as now, a road existed between Clare and Long Melford. Long Melford became a road junction from which roads linked our area to London, St Albans and Colchester. These were three of the oldest and largest of the 50 or so towns built by the Romans in the early years of their occupation.

The economic benefits from membership of the Roman Empire brought prosperity. Key ingredients in this were a common language in Latin, Roman currency and a first class network of roads and security. Cavendish played its part and various finds over the years provide evidence of Roman influence. There are Roman bricks built into the north wall of the church, probably taken hundreds of years ago from the ruins of a Roman villa.

A Roman amphora (two-handled container for wine or oil) and brooch were found in 1958 when work was being undertaken on a sewer trench in the High Street. Elsewhere pottery sherds have also been found as has a Roman coin in a garden in Lower Street.

In the middle of the fourth century life became less settled. Civil war in the Roman Empire hampered the effectiveness of the Roman legions and for the first time East Anglia was attacked by bands of pirates from across the North Sea. The response by the Roman authority proved to be effective and a line of forts was established along the east coast known as the 'Saxon Shore'. In 369 AD peace and prosperity were restored.

In 409 AD the Roman army was recalled and the Britons entered a period of uncertainty and vulnerability. In 428 AD the British chief Vortigern invited the Saxon leader Hengist to send mercenary troops to protect Britain from raids by Picts from Southern Scotland. Between 430 and 441 AD the Saxons took advantage and ravaged and plundered the whole of Britain. They gained control of two thirds of the country with their power base at its strongest in East Anglia. The Roman and British civilisation was almost totally destroyed.

By 500 AD six Saxon Kingdoms had been formed. Around this time the permanent settlement now known as Cavendish became established. It is said that an Angle or Saxon named Cafa owned an edisc or pasture here and the community which developed was known as Cafa's edisc, which eventually became Cavendish. Cavendish was in 'East Anglia' i.e. present day Suffolk and Norfolk plus part of Cambridgeshire where a series of dykes formed a border with the state of Mercia.

Between 500 and 870 AD East Anglia was ruled mainly by a Swedish Dynasty known as Wuffingas. One of them Raedwald, who is thought to have been buried at Sutton Hoo, became 'Bretwalda' i.e. chief King of All England in 617 AD.

In 630 AD a priest from Burgundy was appointed by Raedwald's son to the Diocese of East Anglia, to preach Christianity. The priest was Bishop (later Saint) Felix. Also working in the area was the Irish monk Bishop Fursey. By the late 7th century most settlements had churches but since they were mainly built of timber it is unlikely that evidence of these early churches survives.

The Kings of East Anglia were noted for their holiness and three of them were saints and martyrs – Siegbert (634 AD); Ethelbert (792 AD) and Edmund (870 AD). The first two were killed by Mercians and Edmund by the Danes. The shrine of Edmund became a place of pilgrimage and later the site of the Abbey at Bury St Edmunds.

The Danes who arrived in 865 AD began to settle in the region. By the late 9th century markets were in existence at Dunwich, Ipswich, Bury St Edmunds and Sudbury. More churches were established and so by the time of the Domesday Survey in 1086 over 400 churches in Suffolk were founded. This represents approximately 80% of our surviving medieval churches.

Britain was still fending off its invaders. Ethelred, the King, tried to buy them off but this only increased the belief that Britain had riches worth taking. Ethelred died in 1016. Over the next fifty years the crown changed hands five times eventually passing in 1066 to Harold, the leading earl in the country, who declared himself to be king. Later, in the same year, William of Normandy invaded and Harold was defeated and killed in the Battle of Hastings. It is said that a deacon from Cavendish called Edric also died in the battle.

THE MANORS

William the Conqueror was crowned King of England on Christmas Day 1066. He was keen to reward those who had helped him but also to retain the manorial system which was in place before he came to power. The King owned all the land and gave large parcels of it to his supporters, in return for service. The Lords of the Manor not only owned land but also had authority over a district. They in turn divided the land among their tenants such as freemen, villeins and serfs, who paid in the form of service or work. Serfs or slaves were bought and sold with the manor when it changed hands.

William was keen to record all the taxable holdings in the country and so the idea of the Domesday Survey was born. Clerks were sent to each part of the country to detail the taxable units in each hundred. These could include land, buildings, plough teams, pasture and pannage. (The latter was a payment made by tenants for the right to feed pigs in the manorial woods). Some land and buildings were not listed because they were owned by religious houses and so were exempt from taxation. The annual value of a unit was assessed plus changes which had taken place over the previous twenty years. The survey was completed in 1086, and the entries were grouped under landholders. A parish, therefore, may appear under a number of owners and with different spellings of its name depending on the clerk who took down the information.

Cavendish was spelt in many different ways. Some extracts are:-

> **Kanavadis** is half a league long and four furlongs broad. (A league was three miles and a furlong 220 yards).

> At **Kanavadisc** Norman held with soke and sac under King Edward as a manor 2 carucates of land. A church with 3 acres of land. Then as now 5 villeins and 8 bordars and 7 serfs. Then 2 ploughs on the demesne afterwards and now 4. Then as now 3 ploughs belonging to the men. And 1 mill. And 10 acres of meadow. Then 3 beasts now 24. Then 40 sheep now 110. Then 30 swine now 50.

> Soke and sac -   a jurisdiction claimed by lords as part of their manorial tenure. It included a right to hold a court, and to receive manorial profits and services.

> Carucate -   120 acres

Villein - an unfree tenant holding his land in return for certain agricultural services and fines.

Bordar - had some land for subsistence but had to perform agricultural and menial services for the lord for a fixed sum or for free.

Serf - the lowest status in the hierarchy and could be sold especially when a manor changed hands.

Demesne - land of the manor held by the lord himself. Villeins had to work regularly on the demesne lands in return for their own holding.

In **Kanavdisc** Ralph de Limesi holds a freeman formerly under Harold which Edric the deacon, who died with him in the battle, held … Now Ralph de Limesi holds it in the hall demesne.

In **Kavanadisc** Aluric, brother of the aforesaid Edric encroached upon half his brother's land 60 acres.

At the time of the Domesday Survey the manor of Overhall was held by Ralph de Limesi. It had been assigned to him by William the Conqueror after the Battle of Hastings. Ralph was a nephew of William's and had married a great niece of the previous king, Edward the Confessor. Other lands, not yet forming manors, were owned or held by Richard, son of Earl Gislebert, Roger de St Germains and Richard of Clare.

Over subsequent years these lands were formed into manors through sale, marriage or pieces taken by the king. At one time Cavendish had thirteen manors which is a very large number for a small village. Later as the landowners acquired more land the separate identities of some of these manors became lost as they were subsumed under the larger holdings. Sadly the exact location of many of these manors is not known. Peche's or Pechy's Manor, Peyton's Manor, New Hall Manor and Kensing's or Kessings Hall Manor became part of Colts Hall Manor. Bulley Hall Manor became part of Nether Hall Manor in 1753 and then later about 1826 was sold to the Houghton Hall Manor. Impey or Impsey Manor became part of Houghton Hall Manor in 1626. More Hall Manor, Collingham Hall Manor and Stansfield Hall Manor were in existence in the early 17th century but after 1637 no more is known about them.

Overhall Manor was the original manor house of Cavendish and was given to Ralph de Limesi after the Battle of Hastings by his uncle William the Conqueror. The estate remained in the de Limesi family for 200 years and then through the marriage of a daughter, Basilia, passed into the hands of the de Odingsells (or Odingseles). John Odingseles had a daughter, Alice, who married Sir John Cavendish. John Odingseles died in 1353 and Sir John Cavendish became Lord of the manor through his marriage. Sir John Cavendish was Chief Justice to the Kings Bench under Richard II. During the King's reign Wat Tyler led a rebellion against heavy taxation. He is said to have been killed by Sir John's son, also called John. The mob, in their anger, seized Sir John and he was beheaded in 1381. The manor passed down through the Cavendish family until 1569 when William Cavendish sold it to Robert Downes of London.

The manor eventually passed to Bridget Cracherode in 1601, whose mother Mary is said to have been a daughter of the Cavendish Smiths who had married into the Cavendish family. At this time structural changes to the building were undertaken. Various members of the gentry owned the manor subsequently. In 1767 part of the building was used for the care of smallpox victims, hence the nickname which is sometimes still used today – Pockey Hall.

In 1791 the property was bought by Thomas Ruggles a bencher of Lincoln's Inn. His son, of Spains Hall, Finchingfield took the name Brise and was High Sheriff of Suffolk in 1829. The Ruggles Brise were said to be the lords of the 'Manor of Cavendish' in 1855 and the Yelloly family of Cavendish Hall were said to own the manors of Overhall and Nether Hall. Between 1862 and 1947 Overhall was owned by the Church. In the grounds a new rectory was built to replace the previous one in the High Street which much later became the headquarters for the Sue Ryder Foundation.

Overhall when it was the rectory

After the erection of the new rectory the old Overhall received very little attention and it was decided to pull it down since the costs incurred in keeping it well maintained were considered to be too great. In 1895 old Overhall was demolished. All that remains today is the gable end of the building standing in the grounds of 'new' Overhall.

In a prominent position near the church stands **Nether Hall**. Its timber framing demonstrates Tudor origins, although there has been a manor house on this site for a thousand years. According to Copinger in his 'Manors of Suffolk' 1905, Margaret, wife of Roger de Trehaupton held lands here in 1275. It seems that later on part of the manor was sold without licence and passed on through the Trehaupton family. In spite of their failure to gain permission the 'trespass' was pardoned in 1343 and John de Trehaupton was permitted to retain the land.

The manor at this time comprised 51 acres of land, $1^1/_2$ acres of pasture and $2^1/_2$ acres of wood. Before his death in 1350 John granted the manor to William de Genevyll. Residents of Cavendish will recognise this name from Genevyll Close which was given to a recent development of starter homes in the village.

William died leaving two married daughters, and the manor appears to have passed down through their families for the next hundred years.

Nether Hall

In 1543 the manors of both Nether Hall and nearby Overhall were held by George Cavendish, gentleman usher to Cardinal Wolsey. It appears that after some settlement around this time the manors were again owned separately – Overhall remaining with the Cavendish family until 1569, and Nether Hall passing to the Wentworth family. In 1588 part of the manor came to Matthew Cracherode and Mary his wife, daughter of John Smith of Cavendish. At the turn of the century the Cracherodes also had Overhall. In 1622 the manor of Nether Hall was sold and in 1706 belonged to John Moore of Kentwell Hall who also owned Houghton Hall at this time. The Moores owned the manor until 1826.

Although he did not own the manor, Ambrose Smith is listed as the occupier of Nether Hall in the 'Apportionment of Tithe Rent Charges' of 1846. He was the founder of the Ambrose Smith Charity and in 1869 gave the tenor bell to St Mary's church. His wife Matilda gave the church clock in 1871.

The manor and that of Overhall were owned by the Yelloly family in the mid 19th century. Tom Ambrose moved into Nether Hall on his marriage and it is here that his son Basil was born.

Colts Hall originally known as 'de Grey's manor' is sited about a mile and a half north west of the village and near the highest point of Cavendish. Evidence shows that the site has been occupied from early medieval times. The hall indicates many phases of construction, with parts of the earliest structure (a solar, cross wing, rafters and a crown post) visible in an area of the building which is dated between 1300 and 1350. A two storey wing was added in about 1500 and then around 1650 the rebuilding of the oldest part was undertaken. At this time it seems that additional timbers from elsewhere were introduced. In approximately 1750 and 1830 further remodelling work took place with many of the components recycled and more rooms added. All this makes for a very complex but interesting building.

In 1086 there is reference to an estate in Cavendish belonging to Roger St Germain, one of the vassals of Richard Fitz-Herbert of Clare. Roger came from St Germain in Normandy, near to one of the strongholds of Richard Fitz-Herbert suggesting that the two had links before they came to England. In 1090 Roger is referred to as one of the de Clare's 'barons and other faithful men' who gave to the Clare's new monastic foundation. It is thought that the main residence of the St Germains was at Colts Hall.

By the 13th century, William de Grey owned the estate on which he had a grant of free warren. This meant that the Crown had granted him a franchise allowing him to kill or keep game and beasts. William's son, Sir John de Grey inherited the estate and he had also gained part of the estate of Overhall manor through his marriage to Margaret, daughter of Sir William Odingseles.

The de Greys are thought to be descendents of an Auschetil de Grai who came over with William the Conqueror. Sir John was grandson of Henry de Grey who was said to be a great favourite of Richard I and his successors John, and later Henry III.

The manor passed to Sir John's son Thomas who had married Alice, the daughter and sole heiress of Sir Richard de Cornherd, a knight. In 1321 Thomas and his wife held lands across a wide area including Great Cornard, Little Cornard, Bures, Newton, Waldingfield, Preston and Bardardiston. On Thomas' death, his son Roger succeeded but after he died in 1371 and his own son Thomas, a minor, inherited, the manor was passed through many hands and for a time was held by the Crown.

By 1464 the manor was vested in Thomas son of Thomas Colt of Carlisle and it is from him that the land acquired the name Colts Hall. Thomas Colt was said to be a favourite of Edward IV and after Thomas' death in 1474 the manor passed through seven generations of Colts.

In the time of George Colt, in February 1600, Colts Hall was visited by Will Kemp, author of 'Kemps Nine Daies Wonder'. Will was a comedian and actor in Elizabethan England and at over 50 years of age laid bets that he could dance the 'Morrice' all the way from London to Norwich. On the 20th February he spent three nights at Colts Hall.

He wrote 'At Melford, divers Gentlemen met mee, who brought me to one Master Colts, a very kinde, and worshipful Gentleman, where I had unexpected entertainment till the Satterday. From whose house having hope to somewhat to amend my way to Bury, I determined to goe by Clare, but I found it to be both farther and fouler'.

After the death of another George Colt in 1658 the manor passed to his son, Sir John Dutton Colt MP who sold the manor.

The Manor was bought by the Jennens family of Acton Place and for the first part of the 18th century was occupied by the Ereth family who farmed the land and were copy holders (a form of tenancy). In 1798 William Jennens died. He was said to be the richest commoner in England. As he had failed to sign his will there were many claims to his estate which took many years to resolve. It is said that the dispute formed the basis of Jarndyce v. Jarndyce, which featured in Charles Dicken's book 'Bleak House'.

Eventually after much litigation lasting over 80 years, the estate passed to Richard William Curzon, Earl Howe, a distant relation and then on through the Curzon family. During the latter part of the 19th century, Samuel Viall and later

THE MANORS

Colts Hall   *Denise Davies*

his son Alfred Pratt Viall were tenant farmers at Colts Hall. They were very involved in village life, Alfred at one time being trustee of the Grammar School.

In 1903 Colts Hall passed to Richard the 4th Earl Howe. In 1916 the hall was bought by the great uncle of the present owner. For nearly a thousand years the estate of Colts Hall has remained mainly in the ownership of just five families.

Houghton Hall is situated at the edge of the village on the road to Clare and is reached by a long private drive.

It is mentioned in the Domesday Book as a manor with two carucates of land (one carucate is 120 acres) with soke (jurisdiction) and 1 villein, 2 bordars and 5 serfs. There had been 3 ploughs on the lord's own land and these had increased to 4, and also half a plough belonging to the men. There was woodland for 20 swine (pigs), 10 acres of meadow and 1 horse at the hall. Previously there had been 3 beasts but at the time of the survey there were none.

The house is a listed building and dates from the late 15th century with timber structures of this period. The layout of the building suggests the usual medieval pattern of hall and two cross wings. Alterations were made to the house in the late 16th century and a new roof was added. Further work was undertaken in 1854 when a Georgian front was created.

13

In 1548 Lord of the Manor was Sir John Wentworth of Codham and the manor then passed to his daughter and heir, Anne. She was married three times and inherited the manors of Wiston, of Overhall and Netherhall in Poslingford, and Houghton Hall, Impeys and Bulley Hall in Cavendish. On her death in 1580 the manor changed hands three more times until it passed to Sir Lumley Robinson of Kentwell Hall. It was later sold to John Moore of Kentwell Hall in 1706 and remained in the Moore family until 1826. Sale particulars of 1842 give details of 'a most desirable freehold estate consisting of the Manor of Houghton, Impey and Bulley Hall, also the Houghton Hall Estate and six hundred and sixty nine acres, two rods and thirteen perches.' It belonged in 1885 to George H Goodchild. The property was sold in 1906 to Mr Robert Miller and then to Mr A J Dixon in 1912. The farm was bought by the Wise family in 1938 who have remained there since.

Houghton Hall

FAMILIES

Every village has its individuals and families who contribute to the life of the community. They give of their time, or money or special skills. They make lasting improvements to the facilities available for those living, working or playing here.

Many individuals are mentioned in these pages but sometimes families over more than one generation have had an impact. A few families have been included here to reflect the part played by many over the centuries.

It would not make for interesting reading to detail family trees as little more can be told about all the individual members. Therefore it would seem more appropriate to select some individuals from these families and to begin to identify their links with Cavendish or influences on the wider world.

According to Copinger in his 'Manors of Suffolk', Sir John **Cavendish** was a native of the parish and descended from a branch of the Gernon family who after settling in the village assumed the name Cavendish. Sir John had married Alice Odingseles and through his marriage became Lord of the Manor of Overhall after his father's death in 1353. Sir John was Chief Justice of the Court of the Kings Bench and in 1380 was elected Chancellor of the University of Cambridge. There was insurrection at the introduction of poll tax after a period of economic hardship and Sir John was given the task of suppressing the rebellion. His second son, also called John, was in London with the young Richard II and the Lord Mayor of London when they met with the rebels led by Wat Tyler at Smithfield. Wat Tyler is said to have lost his temper and made a lunge at the Lord Mayor with a dagger. Concerned that his King was in danger the young John Cavendish killed Wat Tyler. He was knighted by the king. The news of the killing incensed the local rebels led by John Wrawe. They captured the older Sir John and dragged him to Bury St Edmunds where he was beheaded in 1381. In his will Sir John left money for needy 'decrepits', the blind, old and others unable to write. In addition he left £40 for the building of the chancel in the church.

After many generations the Manor passed to George Cavendish who was gentleman usher to and biographer of Cardinal Wolsey. One of George's grandsons was Michael Cavendish, the Elizabethan musician who wrote madrigals. A book by him dated 1598, 'at Cavendish', was discovered in 1918 and placed in the British Museum.

George Cavendish's younger brother William (1505 – 1557) took part in the suppression of monasteries and was Treasurer of Chamber to Henry VIII, Edward VI and Mary I. He was married three times and his third wife was Bess of Hardwick whom he married in 1547. She herself had four husbands but it was only with her second husband, William Cavendish, that she had children. It is from William and Bess that the Dukes of Devonshire were descended. Their son William, the first Earl of Devonshire (1552 – 1625), sold the manor in Cavendish in 1569 to Robert Downes of London. It was William's great grandson who was created Duke of Devonshire in 1694.

Another branch of the Cavendish family, who lived at Trimley St Martin, Suffolk, had a son called Thomas born in 1552. It is through him that another link with the village of Cavendish was forged. Thomas became a sailor and led a fleet of ships to Virginia, America. He later became the second man to circumnavigate the world. He was knighted by Queen Elizabeth I, and on another voyage became ill and died in 1592.

In 1913 there was a plan to name six new battle cruisers after famous explorers and Cavendish was chosen as one. After an incident in the First World War, when HMS Vindictive was lost, this name was selected in preference to Cavendish.

Eventually in 1944 a new destroyer was named Cavendish. After a refit in 1956 she was given a new ship's bell inscribed "HMS Cavendish 1956." She was scrapped in 1967 and the bell was presented to the village. It now hangs over a bronze tablet, in the Memorial Hall, on which are recorded the names of those villagers who gave their lives during the First and Second World Wars and the Cyprus conflict.

The present Duke of Devonshire is the eleventh to bear that title. Although the family seat is at Chatsworth, built by Bess of Hardwick, the Duke retains a keen interest in Cavendish since his family's links 'go back a long way'. He has made a number of visits to the village including one in 1973, for the Cavendish Festival Week, when funds were being raised for church repairs. He also visited Manor Cottages to see the Cavendish/Smith coat of arms in the ceiling. In June 1979 he unveiled the new village sign which has the Cavendish coat of arms on one side, and a depiction of the scene during the Peasant's Revolt when Wat Tyler was killed by John Cavendish, on the other.

The Duke also came to open the newly refurbished cricket pavilion on 29th May 1988. He travelled down the High Street from Nether Hall in an open landau drawn by two horses. After the opening ceremony he watched a game of cricket between Cavendish, Suffolk and Cavendish, Australia.

The **Colt Family** originated in Scotland with many estates north of the border.

The Duke of Devonshire at the opening of the refurbished cricket pavilion 1988

It is said that one of the Colts, a border chief, fled south seeking safety after his father was murdered by another family member. He married an heiress near Carlisle and it is from him that the English Colts descended. The influence of this family was not just on the places where they lived but also of a more national and international nature. The Colt family history is long and complex but it is known that eight generations of Colts lived at Colts Hall, Cavendish.

The family also owned many lands in Essex, including Nether Hall at Roydon. The first Colt who lived at the hall in Cavendish in 1464, then known as de Greys, was Thomas, son of Thomas Colt of Carlisle. This son was Chancellor of the Exchequer to Edward IV and also member of the Privy Council. It was after Thomas that the house began to be called Colts Hall.

Thomas' son John married twice. By his second wife he had seven children, two sons and five daughters. His eldest son, George, was knighted and he and his wife Elizabeth are buried in Cavendish church. His sister Jane married Sir Thomas More, who became Lord Chancellor of England. In their short marriage she bore him four children, three girls and the youngest, a son. She died soon afterwards. Sir Thomas More married a second wife, Alice, and it is she who visited him in the Tower of London when he was awaiting execution for refusing to take the Oath of Supremacy after Henry VIII's divorce from Catherine of

Aragon. Another sister, Mary, married William Kemp of Spains Hall, Finchingfield, which later became the home of the Ruggles-Brise family.

In 1578 Elizabeth I is known to have visited Melford Hall, home of Sir William Cordell, where she was entertained to an extravagant reception. It is said that during one of her 'progresses' she visited Colts Hall.

Colts Hall was passed down through three other members of the Colt family until it reached George Colt who had married Elizabeth, daughter of John Dutton. They had nine sons and one daughter. George and his family supported Charles I whilst the Duttons supported the parliamentary cause, which must have caused a certain amount of family tension! George continued to support Charles II, selling part of his Cavendish property to help to fund the cause. Whilst away on King's business he was sailing aboard a Dutch vessel which sank. He was drowned at sea in January 1658.

George Colt's tomb in St Mary's church   *Denise Davies*

His son John Dutton Colt, MP for Leominster, inherited the manor and later sold it.

There was an American branch of the family who were also descended from the Scottish Colts. It was one of them named Samuel Colt who was born in Hertford, Connecticut in 1814 who attained world-wide fame as the inventor of the revolver pistol.

The **Garrett** family with its many members began to have impact on village life from the early half of the 19th century.

Joseph Stammers Garrett

Joseph Stammers Garrett was born in 1813 and was brought up as a farmer and maltster. He was also a merchant carrying on an extensive business for many years in Suffolk and Essex as well as in London. He bought Blacklands Hall Estate in 1853, from Colonel Sir Samuel Ruggles-Brise CB, and lived there until his death. Joseph was one of the leading agriculturalists in the district, farming extensively in Cavendish and the surrounding area for 40 years. He leased one farm from Mr J G W Poley of Boxted Hall, another from the Right Hon. Earl Howe and rented one from Mr Yelloly. These along with his own 900 acres made up a large estate of some 1400 acres, most of it being first class land with the picturesque residence of Blacklands at its centre.

He carried on a large business as a maltster, miller and corn merchant. He was well known at local markets and was considered a very shrewd man of business. He also owned three Maltings in Cavendish, one at Sudbury and for some time hired one at Chilton near the Maldon Grey. In about 1893 he handed over the Maltings to his son Samuel.

He took a deep interest in the projected extension of the local railway line from

Sudbury to Cambridge. Through his persistent support, and that of his friends, the line did become established. As he had predicted the railway proved of great benefit to the area and was financially successful.

Joseph was a staunch Nonconformist. He built the Congregational Chapel (now United Reformed Church) at Cavendish and built the lecture hall (now the Memorial Hall) which was used as the British School. He owned The Old Rectory, now the Sue Ryder Home.

Until Gladstone framed his Irish Home Rule Bill, Joseph had always been a member of the Liberal Party. He felt unable to follow Gladstone on the Irish question and did not hesitate to join the Liberal Unionist Party to which he remained attached until the day he died.

Joseph was placed in the Commission of the Peace for the County of Suffolk, taking his seat at the Melford and Clare Benches. At over 80 years of age he was still attending markets, transacting business, displaying his usual mercantile pursuits as well as managing his large estate.

Joseph was considered a wonderful man for his age with a cheerful disposition. He was married twice and the father of 5 sons and 7 daughters. He was 86 years old when he died in 1899.

Henrietta Garrett was the eldest of the 12 children of Joseph Stammers Garrett and was born in August 1851. In March 1869 she was enrolled as a member of the Cavendish Congregational Chapel, having been transferred from the chapel at Braintree where she and her sisters were at school. She knew all the twelve pastors who had been at the chapel since its inception. Her life was bound up with the chapel activities and her name regularly appears in the chapel records.

For 55 years she was the chapel organist, only retiring at the age of 78. The organ was given by her. She was honorary treasurer of the chapel funds, laid the foundation stone for the manse in 1892, and was instrumental in persuading her father to build the lecture hall, now the Memorial Hall. For many years she acted as delegate to the Suffolk Congregational Union and frequently to the Congregational Union of England and Wales.

She originated and worked a coal club, penny bank and library in Cavendish and was a prominent member of the Dorcas meeting, acted during the Second World War as treasurer to the local War Savings Association and from its start until a few years before her death was treasurer and secretary of the Cavendish and Glemsford Nursing Association.

She would sit at the Memorial Hall taking the penny bank savings money and

Henrietta Garrett

presented quite a daunting figure as described by one Cavendish gentleman. She worked with her brother Samuel at the Cavendish Maltings and would sit at the high stool attending to the books. Towards the end of her life she started to lose her memory and many a person had to turn her around in Water Lane, reminding her that she now lived in Western House. Her long life was full of activity and she was always happy when busy. She died in 1944 at the age of 92.

Samuel John Garrett was born at Blacklands Hall in 1867. He was Honorary Secretary for the local celebrations in connection with Queen Victoria's Jubilee in 1897 and again for the coronations of King Edward VII, King George V and King Edward VIII.

Samuel had precarious health in his younger days and was educated by a private tutor. Later he had a year's experience in the milling industry at Nayland, probably with an uncle on the Stammers side, after which he returned to Cavendish at about the age of 18 and joined his father's business.

In 1898 he and his sister Henrietta took over the malting and milling whilst his father carried on as a farmer.

For 21 years Sam was the chairman of Cavendish Parish Council, but his greatest interest was in the Cavendish Flower Show of which he was the secretary from its inception in 1908. Until it closed some time before 1937 he was a manager of the old British School (at the Memorial Hall). He always supported the village sports organisations and was for some years captain of the Cavendish Cricket Club. He had to have a runner when at the wicket as he had one leg shorter than the other, thought to have been due to an accident in early childhood. In 1937 he assumed the duties of honorary treasurer of the local committee entrusted with the arrangements for the Wickhambrook Show.

Samuel had a great sense of humour and was an extremely kind man. He is on record as being the only person answering a request for donations for the repair of Belchamp Otten windmill following a gale. Once during election time he, along with men at the Maltings, collected up a number of chickens belonging to a staunch supporter of one of the political parties and tied ribbons 'of the wrong colour' on their legs. At that time chickens roamed the village.

Samuel married Kate Ada Bird whose father was at the Brick Kiln Works owned by Joseph Stammers Garrett. She was well known for the prominent and active part she played in the work of the Women's Institute, the Cavendish Dramatic Society and the Cavendish Choral Society. Katie died in 1950 and Samuel in 1955.

They had one son, John William Garrett who married Kathleen Barltrop, daughter of the village blacksmith. They had three children, John, Margaret and Frances all of whom still live locally.

Three generations of Garretts welcoming guests at Cavendish House

The **Ambrose** family have lived in the village for over 300 years. They were yeoman farmers and have always taken an active interest in village affairs. The Local Government act of 1894 authorised the establishment of elected Parish Councils and **Thomas Edward Ambrose** became the first chairman of the Cavendish Parish Council.

His son **Tom** was born in 1890 at Wales Farm and attended Cavendish Grammar School where in 1904 he became the head boy. He developed a life long love of the game of cricket and used to act as scorer for the Cavendish Cricket Team at the age of 10. He was a good fast bowler and was picked to play for Suffolk in 1914 but the First World War intervened, and by the time the team was re-formed after a long break in 1935, he felt he was too old.

He first played for Cavendish in 1905. He later became captain and held the post until 1957. He played his last match in 1961 at the age of 70, but continued to be involved with the club until his death in 1977.

Tom farmed at Scotts Farm, Wales Farm, Wales End and Nether Hall. He managed Blacklands Hall farm for his friend Dudley Payne. He married Nellie and they moved into Nether Hall.

He was on the Cavendish Parish Council for over 50 years and its chairman for 30 years. He resigned in 1973 but during this period he oversaw and initiated many changes in the village, and worked tirelessly to improve its appearance and amenities and the daily life of its people. He was widely known as 'Mr Cavendish'. Under his leadership Cavendish won the Walter Horne Trophy, on two successive occasions, for Suffolk's Best Kept Village.

He helped to lead negotiations for the purchase of the Congregational or British School so that it could be used as the village hall.

It was Tom who initiated the scheme to buy and restore the dilapidated cottages on the green. He and some friends purchased the cottages and after a major fundraising drive the work was completed. The cottages were handed over to the George Savage Trust of which he was the chairman.

When the cottages burnt down in 1971 Tom vowed 'If it is the last thing I do they will be rebuilt'. The cottages were rebuilt after further fundraising and Tom went on to enjoy a further six years in Cavendish.

Basil Ambrose, Tom's son was born at Nether Hall and attended the village school until the age of nine. He then went to boarding school but looked forward to his visits home and the holidays when he enjoyed trips to the Cavendish cinema, playing around the village and observing the activities of the people.

Tom Ambrose with Sir Leonard Cheshire & Lady Ryder

On leaving school he went to Durham University. He was called up for National Service and was directed into the National Agricultural Advisory Service and served there until 1947. On his return to Cavendish he took up farming with his father and was also engaged in specialised agricultural businesses.

In 1947 he was asked to join the Memorial Hall Committee and worked alongside others until 1997 to ensure the development and maintenance of facilities at the hall for the benefit of the whole community.

He was chairman of the Parish Council and on his father's death continued the family tradition of a care for the community.

Basil retired early but was keen to take on a new project. As a wine lover, with experience of farming and an interest in history he decided to explore the possibilities of viticulture in Cavendish. If the Romans grew vines in Eastern England then why couldn't he? Basil went on to establish his vineyard in 1972 which was a success. In 1990 Basil ceased vinifying but continued to sell wine for a period afterwards from cellar stocks.

Basil Ambrose

Like his father Basil has a keen interest in preserving the heritage of the village and in 1994 set up a trust to ensure the long term survival of the Memorial Hall, and in 1995 another trust with his friend Maurice Finbow to ensure the long term continuation of sports and recreational facilities in the village.

CHARITIES AND TRUSTS

Over the centuries benevolent and altruistic individuals have given money to benefit others. Some of the village trusts are long standing and others more recent. A few have been incorporated into other charities and trusts being administered in the village, but the spirit of the original bequest is maintained.

Ambrose Smith directed that on 3rd May, the anniversary of his wedding, £20 should be distributed to 6 men and 6 women of the parish and that the bell ringers should be paid a guinea for ringing on that day. Catherine Stewart Petre's legacy in 1906 was for 'two poor single women of blameless conduct of Cavendish aged 50 years or upwards and members of the Church of England' and £1 per annum for hot cross buns on Good Friday for Sunday School children and teachers. Mary, the daughter of Mr Creane the baker, can remember being involved in both the preparation and distribution of the buns.

The following gives details of some of Cavendish's charities and trusts.

The **George Savage Trust** was set up in 1939 following a bequest made by Mr George Savage. It now has responsibility for the care and maintenance of the five cottages on Cavendish Green known as Hyde Park Corner.

George Savage was born in Cavendish in 1845, one of a family of twelve. His parents, brother Charles and sister Mrs Elsey, all lived beyond the age of 90. His father was a farm worker and George used to recount that when he was too young to walk far, he would be carried into the fields by his father and left to scare birds for a shilling (5p) a week. On many occasions his only food was swedes.

On leaving school he worked on a local farm but soon decided to try his fortune in London. It is said that he left in response to an advertisement in the paper from a woman seeking a partner (whether for marriage or business is not known). He married Emma in 1873 and became the proprietor of an hotel in Waterloo Road in London.

He was successful and in 1883 bought Glemsford Brickyards, 23 acres of land, a dwelling house and cottage in Lower Road, Glemsford. He let the brickyards and some of the rest and over the years acquired further land and properties. He retired to Hill House in Lower Road after 50 years in the hotel business.

Emma, who lost her sight in later years, died in 1924. She was thrown from a trap, driven by her husband, after the pony shied and she never regained consciousness.

George Savage

George lived to the age of 92 and died in 1937. George and Emma had no children and there was great surprise when details of his will were published. Local and national newspapers reported on it with headlines such as 'son of farm worker leaves £29,596'. After bequests to family, friends and charities he left the residue of his estate to Cavendish Congregational Church, 'for the poor and sick of the village and in recognition of the many acts of kindness to my late father and mother shown by the villagers'.

Trustees were appointed and at the first meeting the Trust was registered with the Charity Commission. Mr Tom Ambrose was one of the original trustees and his son Mr Basil Ambrose is still on the committee. The capital sum was invested and the interest received was used to make grants to those in need in the village.

After the Cavendish Preservation Society had purchased, and with help, renovated the Hyde Park Corner Cottages it was decided that they should be handed over to the George Savage Trust. The Trust accepted responsibility for the cottages in November 1957. It was thought that the provision of 'almshouse' accommodation was within the spirit of the original bequest.

There are five dwellings in the group, some with two bedrooms. New residents must be over the age of 60 and have some connection with Cavendish either through family or residence. The maintenance charges are kept at reasonable levels. Seven residents in the village serve as trustees, some of whom are nominated by local councils.

Cavendish Care Meeting November 2001

Denise Davies

CHARITIES AND TRUSTS

Hyde Park Corner Cottages before renovation

Cavendish Care was initiated in May 1987 by Daphne Pawson and Rev. David Deans to provide a transport, shopping or visiting service to the elderly, ill or housebound in the village. A weekly coffee morning was planned in order to offer companionship and social activities. The hostess provided the venue and refreshments.

Since its inception these activities have continued with volunteers providing transport for hospital, doctor and other appointments. Villagers have offered their homes as venues for the weekly coffee mornings and outings have been arranged – to the seaside in summer and for shopping in the run up to Christmas.

Cavendish Endowed School Trust derives from the Grammar School and Charity founded in 1696 by the then Rector, the Reverend Thomas Grey. The school closed in 1907 and the premises were sold. The farm at Pentlow which helped to provide income for the school was sold in 1938. The monies from these form the basis of the Cavendish Endowed School Trust.

The rector is the chairman with three other trustees. They meet annually and distribute between £200 and £300 in total each year to applicants.

The fund is used mainly for grants to young people beginning further or higher education.

The Ambrose Cavendish Village Memorial Hall Trust Fund (The Ambrose Trust) was established in 1994 through the generous donation by Basil Ambrose of a sum of money. Since then other sums have been added. The objects of the trust are the provision of funding to ensure the long term maintenance of the structure, fabric and services of the Cavendish Memorial Hall.

This is a capital fund to make safe the long term future of the village hall. The Parish Council are the trustees.

The Finbow-Ambrose Cavendish Village Sports and Recreational Trust Fund (The Finbow-Ambrose Trust) was registered in 1995. Maurice Finbow and Basil Ambrose gave generously to establish it. The purpose of the trust is the provision of a capital fund, the income from which is to be used for continued and continual supply and maintenance of a recreation and sports ground and/or facilities for the inhabitants of Cavendish village. The Parish Council are the trustees.

AGRICULTURE

From the earliest days agriculture provided the main focus for life and work in Cavendish. In years gone by many people owned and worked small parcels of land, all of which were named. Many fields in the village retain their original identity. The origins of many of these field names are unknown, some have obvious connections and others appear to have historical links. The field at Houghton Hall known today as Lost Bit is said by many previous generations to have been where Queen Boudicca and her supporters 'lost one of their battles against the Romans'.

On a field map of Houghton Hall, dated 1778, many of the field names are the same or similar today – Brick Clamp Field, Great Ruffins, Wheat Field Ley, High Field, Oat Field, Great Long Meadow, Little Long Meadow.

In 1794 Henry Roper of Cavendish School drew a map of Blacklands. In those days it comprised 277 acres. Out of sixteen fields listed, only two retain their original name – Wickhamslade and Abbots.

At Colts Hall the 1846 field names bear a close resemblance to those of the present. Little and Great Rockets is now the Rooket. Church Field, First Church Field and Further Church Field are now one and called Church Field. Old Lawns appears to have been corrupted to Larns. New Lawns is now Pond Field.

Due to changes in farming practices many fields have been amalgamated to accommodate larger machinery and therefore several field names have been lost.

The 29th September is Michaelmas Day and this is traditionally at the end of the farming year. Many farm sales took place at this time. In 1906 there was a farm sale locally where the following items were sold.

Wagon	£ 13
Shepherd's Hut on wheels	£ 4-15s- 0d (£4-75p)
Foot Plough by Ransomes	£ 1-10s- 0d (£1-50p)
6ft Binder	£ 9- 0s - 0d

29 Heavy horses including:

Tinker	£24- 3s- 0d (£24-15p)
Bay mare	£14-14s- 0d (£14-70p)
Diamond	£25- 4s- 0d (£25-20p)
Trimmer	£23-12s- 6d (£23-63p)

Cutting the corn with a binder

In the same year at Houghton Hall a sale was held. Ploughs were sold at 42 shillings (£2-10p), a Smyth drill made £25-10s (£25-50p), a hay rake £3-5s (£3-25p), and a 7 hp traction engine by Burrel raised £150. The horses included some pedigree Suffolk mares and the well known Suffolk stallion, 'Cockfield Prince'. Nine shorthorn steers made £10-7s-6d (£10-37p) each. Thirty black faced ewes at 2 years old made 55s (£2-75p) each and sows in pig made £5-10s (£5-50p) each.

Some of the prices from a local farm sale in 1942 are:-

Fordson tractor (new 1940)	-	£170
Smyth drill	-	£ 55
Binder (6ft cut)	-	£ 30
Cambridge Roll by Wards of Long Melford	-	£ 10-10s (£10-50p)
Harvest Elevator by Wards of Long Melford	-	£ 86
Sheep shearing machine	-	£ 4-10s (£4-50p)
Morris 10 hp car 1934 Licensed	-	£ 45

AGRICULTURE

Horses

      Bay mare Bragg 6 years old   -   £130
      Roan gelding Jolly 9 years old -   £ 90
      Chestnut Mare Poppet 5 years old -   £ 27
      Bay mare Depper 9 year old   -   £ 54

The price of second-hand machinery in the year 2000 was £5,500 for a 4 furrow plough; £60,000 for an 18 ft combine harvester; £5.250 for a Lely combi drill whilst a new 100 hp tractor cost £33,000.

Harvest in progress at Colts Hall in 1999   *John Osborne*

Farms were a hive of activity, employing many men, and particularly during school holidays the children worked on the land. Henry Skeemer was born in 1904 and in 1914 when war came, he passed the labour exam which entitled him to leave school and commence work. Recorded in the school log book on 23rd September 1916 is the fact that due to late harvest the school remained closed until 2nd October.

One of the favourite traditions of the farming year was the 'Harvest Home'. A local paper reported on 6th October 1909:

> 'On Friday evening last, all the men numbering 27, who worked on the estate of Houghton Hall were entertained to a bountiful spread' at the Five Bells Cavendish by invitation of the Master, Mr G M Miller Esq. After giving due justice to old English fare, the Master gave from the chair, the loyal toast to the King and the Royal Family, after which Noah

Fitch (Lord of the Harvest) proposed the health of the Master and Mrs Miller and family, to ringing cheers. They then gave the Master the old fashioned song 'for he's a jolly good fellow'.

Ploughing matches proved popular and were held from time to time. In November 1899 a local newspaper reported:-

'A ploughing match was held at Blacklands Hall, Cavendish on Monday. It was the first of its kind held in the parish for many years.

There were three prizes

For men over 30 years.

1st - James Crissel,
2nd - Harry Underwood,
3rd - F Underwood,
4th - T Wells,

The first and second prize-winners work for Mr Ray, third and fourth for Mr Garrett.

Second class - for men over 20 and under 30.

1st - Alfred Brown,
2nd - W Martin,
3rd - Arthur Brown.

The first and second are Mr Garrett's men, the other works for Mr Allen of Houghton Hall.

Third Class for men under 20.

1st - F Fitch, Houghton Hall,
2nd - G Wells, Blacklands.

Judges were S Ewer of Foxearth and Mr W Coldham of Boxted.'

Farming records of 1907 written by W S Maddever of Wales End Farm show 6 men employed. During the spring tasks undertaken included threshing, sacking beans, cleaning mangolds, ditching, spreading muck, twitching (digging out twitch grass from ploughed edge of field), drilling red clover, spreading mole hills, pulling docks and thatching stacks. The total average weekly wage bill was £3-5s-0d (£3.25p).

AGRICULTURE

Howard Maddever was born at Wales End and the family moved to Stanstead Hall in 1922. Howard bought Scotts farm in 1963 and it is now farmed by his son Peter.

Between 1936 and 1941 there were 17 men employed at Blacklands Farm.
>Mr Barnard acted as Farm Manager.
>The workforce was divided into:-
>Horsemen - Mr Bullock, Henry Skeemer, Sam Brown, Mr Ablet, and Harry Parmenter;
>Tractor men - Fred Wells, Ralph Brown and Alfred Brown;
>Stockmen - the shepherd Fred Ives (looking after 200 Suffolk ewes), Don Angel (pig man), boys Adams/John Chatters;
>Maintenance - Mr Amos;
>Day Men - George Skeemer, Buck Skeemer, Hookey Wells, Mr Thompson and Mr Byford.

The total wages bill for a week averaged £35.

Henry Skeemer, horseman outside Blacklands

At Colts Hall during the 1960s four full time men and one part time man were employed. The weekly wage bill in 1965 was £11.50 per man.

In the year 2000 it was calculated that one man would be required to work 350 acres.

Another change which has occurred over the last one hundred years has been the movement from mixed farming to arable. In 1917 it is noticeable that many crops were grown for stock feed as every farm carried livestock. In recent years crop rotation had to be revised as a result of less stock being reared, the demise of the horse as a working animal, and the requirement of the world wide markets.

The following chart demonstrates the trend:

1917	**1941**	**1965**	**2000**
Mixed Clover	Wheat	Wheat	Wheat
Oats	Spring Barley	Spring Barley	Barley
Barley	Rye Grass	Beans	Rape
Wheat	Spring Beans	Clover	
Red Clover	Trefoil	Oats	
Mangels	Red Clover	Grass/Clover (mixture)	
Swedes	Potatoes		
Rye Grass	Turnips		
Turnips	Mangel		
White Clover	Winter Oat		
Tares	Spring Oats		
Beans	Winter Beans		
Peas	Peas		
(Fallow)	Tares (folded-sheep)		

For centuries the **blacksmith** was a most important part of rural life due to the dependence on the horse for power and transport. The blacksmith played a vital role for the farmer, shoeing their horses and repairing machinery. In a directory of 1855 (before the coming of the railway), there are four blacksmiths listed in Cavendish including a woman, Elizabeth Mott. At the same time there were two wheelwrights, a related trade, one being Edward Hardy and the other Boanerges Brown.

In a sale catalogue of 1901 for the contents of wheelwrights and blacksmiths shops in Cavendish, the sum of £40-14s-0d (£40.70p) was made.

Items for sale included:-

    an anvil - £1-5s-0d ((£1.25p);
    blacksmiths bellows and frame - £1;

smiting hammer and eight pairs of tongs - 4s-6d (22½p);
a hundred spokes, chopping block, stool, iron wheel and sundries - 3s-6d (17½p) and
wagon shafts frame, pole and sundries - 6s-0d (30p).

Threshing time

Many village craftsmen were of a family tradition, and so it was with George Barltrop, highly skilled as a farrier and able to repair tools and equipment for local farms and households.

George came to Cavendish from Debden in Essex around 1907. He was the seventh generation to carry on the trade as blacksmith, his four times great-grandfather, Robert, being one of the first known in the early 1700's. George's five brothers were also blacksmiths. As the Cavendish blacksmith's shop was on the main road to Cambridge he was kept very busy shoeing horses for the passing trade as well as for local people. He did in fact advertise his trade in local journals, and in a 'Guide to Cavendish' is listed as an ironmonger supplying general furnishing, shoeing smith and machinist. He was a keen horticulturalist and member of the fire brigade, the manually operated fire engine being stationed in his yard.

At the time of his death in 1961, aged 91, he was the oldest inhabitant of the village and last of the old village craftsmen.

Mr Joe Hale (1912 – 1988), lived in Cavendish all his life. His father was a butcher and he followed him into the business. This account details his memories of Cavendish farms.

> 'Village life was built around the farms, there were so many men employed to what there are nowadays, that the whole village was centred round each farm. In those days most farms employed about 3 men to 100 acres, and a stockman because they had a lot of horses. Nowadays there's about 1 man to 300 acres, so actually there's only 1 man working where there were 9 previously. Starting at the Clare end coming into Cavendish, just over the Clare border towards Cavendish on the left hand side is a long drive, up there about a mile is the farm

Stackyard at Houghton Hall

AGRICULTURE

called **Houghton Hall**. It's quite a large farm, I imagine between 400 and 500 acres. The land mostly joins Clare and Poslingford. In my young days there were 5 or 6 cottages up there and they housed most of the employees at work on the farm, there was also one large cottage that was where the foreman lived. Mr Dixon lived in the farm. The stockman, he was a funny old man, most odd. His father used to teach me at Sunday School, and he used to stay on afterwards to blow the organ for the church service and he would walk home and then down again in the evenings to blow for the evening service. His son, the stockman, when

Shooting party at Colts Hall

he got cross with the pigs, he shouted terribly and when the wind was in the right direction we could hear him quite plainly down in the village, shouting at the cattle and the pigs. From Houghton Hall we come back to **Scotts Farm**, the next farm on the left. Years ago there were a few buildings in front of the Fir Trees which we called **Fir Tree Farm**, but

39

they were all incorporated into Scotts Farm, because they all belonged to the landlord who owned Cavendish Hall. Scotts Farm was farmed by Mr Richardson. He kept a little herd of cows, a lot of pigs, and he used to send milk into the village, although in my young days there was very little milk delivered in the village, it had to be collected. From Scotts Farm we come along the Green and a sharp left up by the church. Facing the church is **Nether Hall Farm**. I used to go there every morning to get milk for my mother. We tapped on the door and the farmer's wife came with a big scoop and measured the milk into our jug. Not a very big farm, but they kept 2 or 3 men. Most of the top end of the village had their milk from there. Then we fork left and about 1½ miles up the road is what used to be called **Ark Farm**, which is now pulled down completely. There used to be 2 small cottages and farm buildings, which belonged to the council and they were let as smallholdings. Ark Farm was about 60 acres. Mr Starling used to be there, an odd chap, he liked his beer. Further on we come up to **Colts Hall**, a large farm of about 500 acres. Its land joins Poslingford. There were three cottages up there, where some of the employees lived, but the rest of the workpeople went up everyday from Cavendish on foot or on cycle. They kept a lot of stock. **Robbs Farm** is next, 1½ miles from Nether Hall along a very poor road. This was about 300 acres, Mr Bettinson lived in Colts Hall house, but he farmed Robbs Farm. The actual owner of Colts Hall lived at Clare. There was a footpath from Robbs to Colts Hall. We used to walk there Sunday afternoon with our dogs and try to catch a rabbit. From Robbs we go to **Wales Farm**, this used to be kept by Mr Ambrose, whose son now lives at Nether Hall, or rather his grandson. About 250 acres. Further on was **Wales End Farm**. That is pulled right down and it's all in with Wales Farm. At the end of the woods was a sharp left turn down to the **Moors**. That is another little farm, which is 2½ miles from the village. A little boy used to walk down to school every morning, all weathers. Left by the Old Chapel we turn to **Blacklands Farm** – this was the farm of Cavendish. When I was a lad, 22 or 23 men worked there. It was owned by Mr Goodchild from Wratting. Mr Death was the foreman. Each week he used to bring the wages cheque to my father to cash. The wages for all those men came to about £28 a week. About half as much as the average wage of one man now. At Blacklands there was ½ a gamekeeper, a shepherd, a thatcher, four horse keepers, a man and a boy looking after the stock. They kept over 20 horses, plenty work for the blacksmiths. From there we go up the Glemsford road, to the left leads to **Ducks Hall** and **Kimson** (that was a little farm in the fields now part of Ducks Hall). Ducks Hall was derelict when I was a boy. An old man named Smith and his son lived there and they only farmed half of it. They used to have pigs killed for themselves, we used to kill them at the shop for them – they were enormous, the biggest ones I ever saw in my life. We've had pigs weigh 520 pounds. Nowadays an average pig killed weighs about 100 pounds. They used to salt the whole sides on the floor, they did not cut them up till they had cured them, by putting layers of salt on the floor, then on the side of pork, and they lay there about 2 months.'

THE WEATHER

Cavendish Weather 1895 & 1995

In 1895 Samuel J Garrett kept a record of the weather in Cavendish, and his account for the year makes fascinating reading. It was recorded at Cavendish House in his garden where Orchard House is now sited; this was a walled garden so his records must take account of this.

Sam's records of 1895 show that snow fell on 16 days in January and on 12 days in February with a fall of 10 cms on 1st February. He reported 'snow during the night, slight snow during the day'. The wettest day recorded was the 21st July with 3.6 cms 'heavy rain during morning, thunderstorms later, followed by bright intervals'. The coldest day was the 6th February with a temperature of -5° C 'very cold, slight snow, very fine, bright later'. The hottest day was the 26th September with a temperature of 28.8° C 'fine, bright and hot'

1895	Mean Maximum ° C	Rainfall mm
January	2.01	61.47
February	1.33	11.43
March	9.55	51.31
April	13.65	38.1
May	17.90	18.29
June	21.33	14.99
July	21.42	110.24
August	21.42	86.61
September	22.69	18.80
October	11.63	69.09
November	10.63	63.5
December	5.93	53.34

THE WEATHER

Michael Pizzey has kindly provided us with his readings for 1995 - one hundred years later.

The equipment used in both records is very similar, Samuel's equipment was made by Negretti and Zambra and is still available today. Samuel's and Michael's rain gauges were both made by Negretti and Zambra and snow tested.

Michael is one of the more than 50 private volunteers across the country who, along with staff on land owned by borough councils, agricultural colleges, airfields and nature conservancy bodies send their readings to the Meteorological Office. The results are fed into their computer and analysed.

Michael has performed this role since March 1977, although he began rainfall measurements in June 1974. Readings and measurements are taken every day and records made of cloud cover, wind direction and speed, visibility, humidity levels, maximum and minimum air temperature for the previous 24 hours, soil temperature to a depth of 30 cm, rainfall (using a 5" rain gauge and a tilting siphon rain gauge) and total sunshine. This data is supplemented by remarks on the daily conditions.

In 1995 the records show that the only significant snow of the year fell in early March (5 cm) with some (3cm) in early December and falls of 4 cms and 2 cms after Christmas.

1995	**Mean Maximum ° C**	**Rainfall mm**
January	7.4	106.5
February	9.4	69.2
March	10.0	55.3
April	14.0	13.3
May	17.5	15.3
June	19.1	20.7
July	25.8	28.0
August	26.2	9.0
September	18.1	140.0
October	17.5	7.8
November	10.4	19.1
December	4.3	69.5

The year was considered to be an average one for rainfall, although January and September were very wet with 106.5 mm and 140 mm recorded respectively. April, May, August and October were relatively dry months. The wettest day of the year was the 15th September when 22.3 mm of rain fell.

There was a very late frost on 14th May when the temperature fell overnight to -2.8°C. There was a cold spell from Christmas Day onwards to the New Year and on the 28th December and 29th December the temperature fell to -8.6°C and -8.3°C.

The hottest day of the year was 1st August when a temperature of 33.2° was recorded. It reached 30.8°C on the last day of June and then for 5 days from 29th July the temperature recorded was above 30°C each day.

i.e.	29th July	30.8° C
	30th July	30.3° C
	31st July	32.0° C
	1st August	33.2° C
	2nd August	30.4° C

Later in August the temperature reached 30° C on another three occasions.

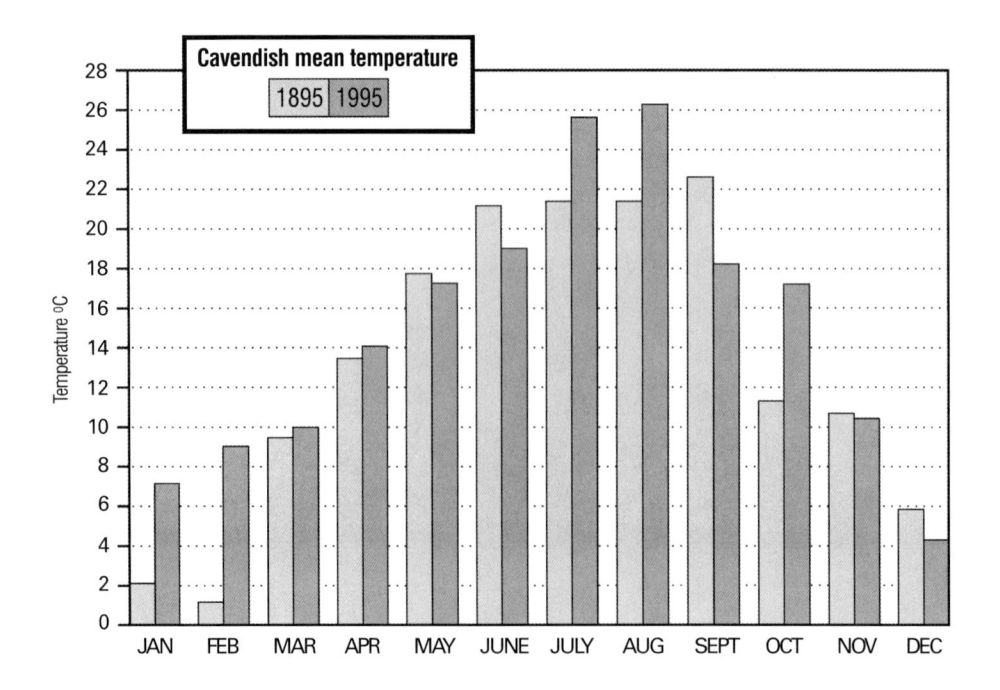

THE WEATHER

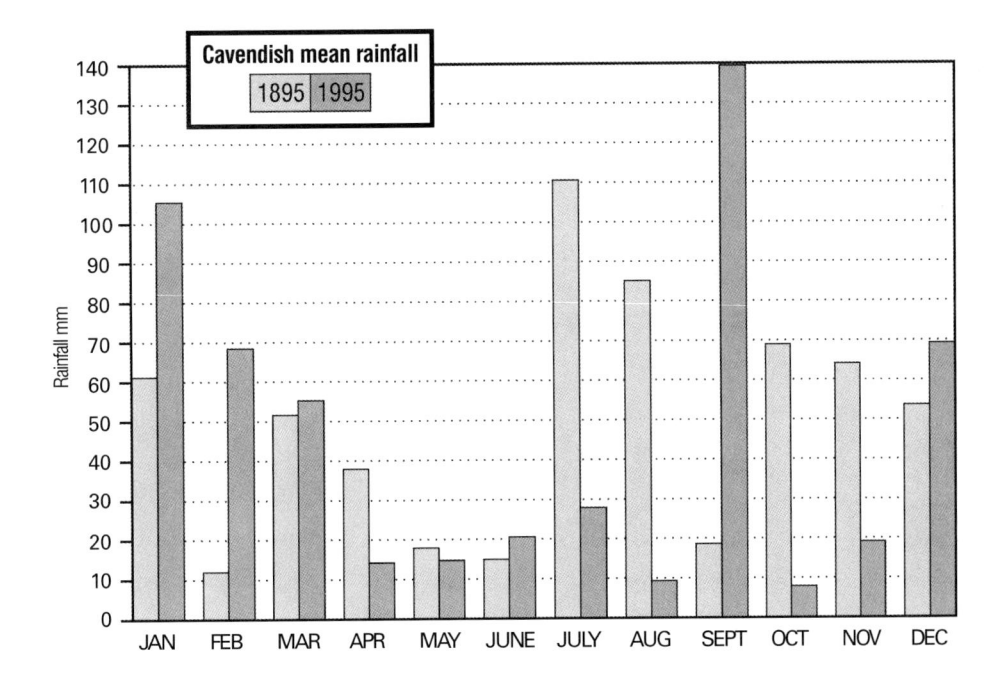

Cavendish mean rainfall
1895 1995

FLORA & FAUNA

Prior to the outbreak of war in 1939 there was an abundance of wild flowers and animals in our countryside. Otters bred in our reach of the River Stour, pheasant and partridge rearing was unheard of and a day's shoot of wild birds was a popular winter sport. Overgrown hedges were a mass of blackberries and a haven for rabbits.

The 1930s were years of depression in farming. Many farms were sold for a pittance or became derelict and empty. Farm power was provided mainly by the cart horse and every farm carried mixed stock and poultry. The rotation of crops took the form of a four year programme of cereal, hay, roots and grazing land. This was environmentally friendly to wild life and flora.

After the outbreak of war in 1939 a War Agriculture Committee was formed by the government. The aim of the committee was to facilitate the maximum farm production of meat, wheat and sugar. The work of the committee was implemented by local representatives within the villages. They had to report on the condition of the agricultural land and what machinery was required to increase food production. Tom Ambrose was the village representative. Water meadows were drained, scrubland ploughed and hedges were removed to assist in the movement of larger machinery. Through the introduction of artificial fertilizers and insecticides and the elimination of cart tracks a large number of seed eating birds and hedgerow flowers were lost.

Hedges

John Constable immortalised Suffolk elm trees in his paintings and together with oak and ash they dominated the skyline above Cavendish hedges. Field maple, hawthorn, blackthorn and occasionally dogwood and spindle filled in the bottom and middle of the hedge giving cover to small nesting birds and mammals. Wild rose and bramble sprawled throughout. The fruit of the blackthorn makes a warming liqueur (sloe gin). The wild rose flower became the emblem for Queen Alexandra's Rose Day annual collection for hospitals, which was founded in 1912 and is Britain's oldest National Flag Day. The hips of the rose were collected during the 1939 war and made into concentrated syrup of vitamin C for children.

The hedge from Embleton House to the avenue above Blacklands has six old elms and oaks. The elms, still struggling against Dutch Elm disease, have successfully suckered along the hedge and their growth is thick and about 10 metres (30 feet) high.

In 1953 a hurricane swept up the valley, lifting chicken huts, demolishing chimneys, and felling many trees. The avenue at Blacklands was blocked with fallen oaks and many elms; a few dead stumps still survive in the hedges today but most of the walnuts in Blacklands Park and about 40 trees at Cavendish Hall and many fine specimen trees throughout the village were lost.

On May 9th 1957, Mr Jack Pawsey of Blacklands together with Mr Westrop and Derek, his son, commenced planting Poplar Robusta on the Glemsford road. This date was confirmed by Mrs Johnson (Millie Westrop). These poplars were used to publicise the 1988 European Tour of Pink Floyd on a poster. An LP record of the tour, which featured the poplar trees and for some reason rows of metal beds on the reverse, was tracked down in a record shop in Prague by Brian Kemp. Mr Anthony Pawsey, Jack's son, has continued planting hundreds of trees 'over the last ten years'.

Along the walk from Embleton House to Ducks Hall, flowers to be found include nettle-leaved bellflower, agrimony, selfheal, cowslip, hedgerow cranesbill and wild garlic

Woodland

The old drover's road from Wales End to Fenstead End has a variety of spring and summer flowers. It has a ditch and bank on the left hand side to the end of the wood. On the right where the agricultural land comes up to the edge of the track the drift of spray diminishes the number of flowers. There are pendulous sedge clumps in the ditch, and cowslip, primroses and teasels along the bank; on the verge are violets, yellow wort, centaury, shepherd's needle and black medick to mention a few. The only butterflies seen here are the small blue, skipper, meadow brown, small white and speckled wood.

Easty Wood is wet with one spring pond and several boggy areas. The ancient history of the wood is demonstrated by the presence of many coppiced ash, hazel and elm stools, one of which is 16 feet (nearly 5 metres) in circumference. All are totally rotten in the centre but have young limbs still reaching skywards.

The north west end is drier and has a plantation of oaks approximately 100 years old for future harvesting. Flowers found here include anemones, primroses, bluebells, and early purple orchids, followed by ragged robin, campion, yellow archangel, agrimony, angelica, goldilocks buttercup and hairy mint. There are several species of sedge (which have edges) and rush (which are round) with an abundance of meadow sweet in the autumn.

In the silence pigeons, pheasants, blackbirds, wrens, robins, tits and warblers are always there with the occasional nightingale in song

Survey of the cart track to the end of Easty Wood – July 1998

Bartsia, red	Basil, wild
Bent, common	Bindweed, field
Bramble	Brome, soft
Buttercup, creeping	Centaury, common
Centaury, white	Chervil, bur
Chervil, rough	Cleaver
Clover, white	Cocksfoot
Cranesbill, cut leaved	Dandelion
Dead nettle, white	Dock, wood
Fluellen, round leaved	Fluellen, sharp leaved
Forget-me-not, field	Grass, black (slender foxtail)
Grass, false oat	Grass, rye (perennial)
Grass, smooth meadow	Gromwell, common
Ground ivy	Groundsel, common
Hemlock	Herb Robert
Hogweed	Knapweed, common
Mayweed, pineapple	Mayweed, scented
Medick, black	Mugwort
Nettle, stinging	Nipplewort
Orache, common	Ox-tongue, bristly
Pansy, field	Parsley, cow
Pimpernel, scarlet	Plantain, broad-leafed
Plantain, rib wort	Primrose
Ragwort	Sedge, pendulous
Self heal	Sow thistle, prickly
Sow thistle, smooth	Sow thistle, perennial
Speedwell, field	Speedwell, wall
Spurge, dwarf	St John's wort, perforate
Teasel	Thistle, creeping
Thistle, spear	Timothy grass
Toadflax, small	Trefoil, hop
Trefoil, lesser	Vetch, tufted
Violet, dog common	Willowherb, great
Wintercress, common	Woundwort, hedge
Yarrow	Yellow wort

FLORA & FAUNA

The River

Coming into the village from Clare, the first view of the River Stour is after it has performed its excessive meander at Pitchers Hole opposite the entrance to Houghton Hall drive. History does not relate the origin of this name. Flowing deep in its bed, it passes through farmland with willow and poplar, ash and oak along its banks. Heron fish for small shoals of perch and roach. Pike are ever present in the murky depths. Kingfishers, flash of blue and orange, nest in the river bank and their piping call informs one of their presence seeking minnow, loach and gudgeon in the river during spring and early summer when the river is low. In time of flood they feed in the Waver (village pond) or Water Lane brook.

A series of deep meanders flow around Cavendish Mill house and Cottage. Here the banks of the river are thick with reed, nettle, purple loosestrife, willow herb, Himalayan balsam and recently introduced giant hogweed with plantations of willow, poplar, ash and old oak on either side. The millpond has been filled in and reed mace, wild iris and marsh marigold thrive. On the bank stands an aged willow. Beside the wooden bridge leading to Bower Hall is a goat or pussy willow bush, gold and silver when in flower in April. Thick ivy and hop cover the bridge rail end and hedge sparrow and chaffinch frequently build within. Lean over the rail and you may see the nose and glassy eye of a pike watching you from beneath a lily pad.

The Craven Family, when they lived at the Mill House, planted up the willow field and cottage garden and the whole area is a wild bird and insect sanctuary with guelder rose, blackberry, spindle, elder and blackthorn and a generous growth of comfrey.

Mr Roy Gibbons saw a barn owl two nights running in the winter of 2000 on the roof of his aviary at Stour View. Green woodpeckers, great spotted woodpeckers, long tailed tits, warblers, wagtail, goldfinch and sparrows are regular garden visitors in Mill Lane.

The river straightens out and it flows languidly down through two meadows before the Hullets Wood on its north bank, which in the spring is a picture of snowdrops, bluebells and red campion. Cormorants occasionally come up river and perch and preen on the overhanging branches of a dead tree. The two fields through which it passes are both vulnerable to flooding, and at these times water overflows into Stour Street opposite the field called the Dallams.

At the end of Weir Field a pipe through the side of the weir takes water into the old course of the River Stour in the summer. Whilst the main river runs on through 'the New Cut' to the sluice gates and through Pentlow Mill, the 'Old

Stour' stream runs sluggishly along the back gardens of Poole Street, sometimes uncomfortably close in winter, and through the grounds of the Sue Ryder Home. The area between the two rivers is mostly overgrown; moles delight in the damp soil and birds sing high in the willow and poplar branches on a June evening, safe from sparrowhawk predators.

Emerging out of its winter swampland the river suffers an identity shock finding itself flowing between the manicured grass banks of the Jackson's garden, where it joins the brook from Water Lane, and together they pass through the old railway cut into the Mill Pool.

The Mill Pool field has the third oldest footpath in the village running alongside a row of Lombardy poplars, planted by Mary Turkentine and Mr Hillier in 1948/9 to shield Pentlow Mill House from the railway line. Three majestic limes stand on the bank by the sluice, which is a carpet of primroses in spring.

The ceaseless fall of water, the superb weeping willows around the mill pool and the sight of a pair of swans as they make their way along the river to the old brick bridge, give this place a peace and tranquillity at any time of the year. Skullcap, of the nettle/mint family is found in the concrete at the edge of the mill pool.

All the trees in the meadow have preservation orders on them and the Soay sheep graze in peace having survived the three months of isolation due to the foot and mouth quarantine, between March and the end of June 2001.

Leaving the millpond, the river is shallow and sparkling down to the red brick bridge which carries the Essex coat of arms dated 1888. Kingfishers flash through the arches, which in the spring of 2001 were filled to within 3 inches of the top by the swollen river. At dusk a large colony of pipistrelle bats feed on midges low over the water, weaving and dipping through the arches. Their roosts are probably in the roofs of Pentlow Mill and church. It was from this bridge that Ray Cooper had a sighting of a pair of otters in February 2000.

Mr Alfred Tharby tells of when he was a young boy and living at the Gate House nearly eighty years ago he cut an ash stick for a fishing rod. When he finished with it he stuck it into the ground behind the old station platform where it rooted and still thrives today.

An aged hawthorn tree marking the end of the station platform grows at the bottom of 10 Pentlow Drive and is of ecological value. It is white with blossom in spring, red berries feed birds in winter and its ivy covered trunks shelter hibernating insects.

FLORA & FAUNA

The Millpool

In 1985 the residents in Pentlow Drive were offered extensions to their gardens into Station Field by the landowner Hugh Chapman. He retained a right of way to Cocktailors field and sold the river side two thirds to Sir Patrick Gillam of Pentlow Hall.

During the winters of 1995, 1997 and 1998 this area was planted with native and ornamental trees as listed below:-

Black poplar	10	Catalpha	1
White willow	5	Flowering cherry	2
London plane	5	Liriodendron	1
Ash	8	Paulownia	1
Lime	11	Ailanthus	1
Maple	2	Wellingtonia	2
Weeping willow	4	Sweet chestnut	1
Beech	4	Evergreen oak	1
Hornbeam	2		

The Village

Cavendish can almost be said to be a village within an arboretum. It is a place where trees have been planted throughout the years and the planting is continuing into this millennium.

> 'Plant a tree in 73
> Plant some more in 74
> Are they alive in 75?'

This ditty accompanied St Edmundsbury Council's policy of donating trees as requested by villages, for planting on roadside banks, village greens and verges. This scheme still continues today.

To the west of the village lies Cavendish Hall with its twin lodges. The lime avenue has survived two hurricanes but the old cedars in the park lost many branches. A fine Scots pine stands on the rise of the lawn. An impressive beech flourishes outside the old stables.

Since Cavendish and its Green are so well known this would seem an appropriate starting point for an exploration of the rest of the flora and fauna of the village.

The twelve mixed deciduous and ornamental trees around the village green are all well established. The two majestic limes at the back of the green together

The road to Glemsford taken from the sleeve of the Pink Floyd European Tour '88 album
(see page 47) *with kind permission of EMI records*

with the small leaved lime, tucked into the corner of the school playground, are considerably older. These and the Wellingtonia Sequoia must be some of the oldest trees in the village. Wellingtonia Sequoia began to be imported from California after 1853.

The variegated maple and the beech at the bottom of the green were planted by Tom Ambrose and Don Angel to commemorate the coronation of Queen Elizabeth II in 1953. A small but aspiring sweet chestnut was planted on the green at the beginning of the walk through to Greys Close by our Chairman of the Parish Council and Tree Warden, Shannon Craig. This was to celebrate the millennium.

At the top of the green stands a horse chestnut tree alongside the children's play area. In the autumn the conkers do not lie on the ground for long here.

Leaving the village green by the footpath alongside the cemetery one enters Peter's Field which together with Rectory Field and Chimneys were chosen by Basil Ambrose for his vineyard. Peter's Field was named after a rector who held the living of Cavendish between 1860 and 1895. A row of red brick cottages stood at the edge of this field. When demolished about 70 years ago one of the chimneys remained long enough for the field to claim its name. Poplars were planted as windbreaks around these fields to provide shelter for the vines.

Basil Ambrose also planted up the glebe land around Nether Hall and towards Manor Close with mixed native and ornamental trees and shrubs.

A poplar just inside Church Close is living evidence of the old pond which was sited at the end of the farmyard of Church Farm. Church Road is lined by prunus and variegated maple.

Entering the churchyard by the kissing gate, a weeping silver birch grows on the ditch bank. Inside 'the church' has planted the ninth yew in the churchyard. This was to mark the millennium. At the eastern end of the churchyard stands a Corsican pine whose girth is 11 feet (335 cm). It is not difficult to imagine it has been there since worshippers first trod the long path past the weeping ash to the church.

On the corner past Hyde Park Corner Cottages and outside Chinnerys stand a lime and an elm. The elm is new growth from the base of a tree which succumbed to Dutch elm disease.

On the grass in front of Sue Ryder's former home the family planted a Cedar Atlantica Glauca in 1970. The long garden with pond, bordered on the south by the old river course has a stately Scots pine by the house. An old quince full of

Bridge over the River Stour *(see page 49)*

fruit this year stands on the side of the lily pond and an ancient small leaved lime overhangs the red brick wall into the garden of Debenhams. A row of beech trees forms a natural barrier between the garden and the wetland of the old river and the row of lime trees bordering the High Street are kept pollarded.

It is not surprising that the village enjoys an abundance of bird life, resident and migratory. The yaffle of woodpeckers and the repetitive call of collared doves, pigeons and rooks are evocative of summer. Green woodpeckers frequent our lawns to dig for ants. Robins, wrens, blackbirds, sparrows, greenfinch, chaffinch, blue tit, great tit and starlings nest in the garden areas and are all regular bird table visitors. A pair of robins nested twice in the garden of the Dower House earlier this year. In winter and spring warblers come in from the riverside.

It is not unusual to see a pheasant or partridge on the lawn or grass snake in your fish pond, or to lose your goldfish to an early morning visit from a heron. Canada geese fly up the valley from their summer home in Glemsford gravel pits.

A brambling visited Chippins in February and March 2001, and a family of great spotted woodpeckers regularly feed on the peanuts there.

In spring up to a dozen long tailed tits arrive in the garden and remove any hibernating greenfly from the rose bushes and a charm of goldfinches pause for a 'newstalk' before scattering to the sloe bushes in the hedgerows.

House martins, swifts and swallows arrive during the first week in May and return to their regular haunts. The swifts nest under the chancel eaves of both St Mary's and Pentlow churches. The swallows and house martins reuse old nests which are scattered throughout the village. The majority leave in the last week in August.

Magpies and jays nest in the 'belts' and in any high vantage point of our hedges, they and the grey squirrel scavenge small bird's nests. Empty pheasant egg shells along a footpath are proof of the end of yet another clutch. Tawny and little owls are frequently heard throughout the village.

A large Corsican pine stands at the junction of Water Lane and Lower Street. It marks the plantation of trees planted in the 18th century along the west side of Blacklands Park. The park, once enclosed on three sides by road, is now subdivided into sports field, agricultural land and a small fenced meadow containing the five remaining walnut trees. The Water Lane plantation suffered hurricane damage but still has several Scots pine, oak and sycamore trees. It has recently become a favoured nesting site for a dozen pairs of rooks. A small copse with beech, oak and sycamore stands alongside Park Cottages, where the Wells family live.

Following the public footpath through Blacklands Hall farmyard, vervain (Verbena Officianalis) can be found in the cracks in the concrete above the pond sluice gate. This has flourished with the wet summer. The water course flows through Blacklands Farm land and the Payne/Pawsey family have planted trees in all the hedges and copses throughout the farm.

A stone pine at the entrance of the old drive is one of a dozen different species of old trees. The drive and plantation are a haven for all birds and small mammals. The undergrowth is thick grass with nettle, bramble and wild rose. A three year old mulberry inside the gate has a Wellingtonia as its neighbour. The old tree has lost its crown and has a full length scar down its trunk from a lightning strike during a thunderstorm. Yew and thuya clutter the back of the old tennis court. Along the side of the drive are dogwood, spindle, berberis, cotoneaster, forsythia, lilac and rhododendron.

Oak, Scots and Corsican pine are a haven for small birds including long tailed tits and the undergrowth provides cover for foxes, rabbits and pheasants.

At the junction of footpaths 18/20 is an ancient holm oak with its close relatives, the variegated gold and silver and common hollies, standing at 12 feet (4 metres) high nearby.

The following list conveys the variety of this plantation and its value to wild life. The plantation was established long ago when a horseman lived at the lodge which had a pony stable and harness room beside it.

Stone pine	Bird cherry
Scots pine	Maple
Corsican pine	Hawthorn
Wellingtonia Sequoia	Elm
Copper beech	Portuguese laurel
Beech	Common laurel
Oak	Spindle
Red chestnut	Dogwood
Sycamore	Mulberry
Ash	Holly (common, silver, gold)
Crab apple	Walnut
Holm oak	

Shrubs

Berberis	Cotoneaster
Forsythia	Lilac
Rhododendron	

Horse chestnuts predominate Melford Road and the Memorial Hall car park. A walk through to the sports field in spring will reveal two lime trees heavy with blossom and alive with bees and insects. The sound of bees collecting the pollen has delighted apiarists John Garrett and Michael Pizzey. On the north side of the sports field is a high maple and hawthorn hedge with larch, oak and beech planted at intervals along it. Together with the two plantations to east and west it is a truly lovely site for recreation.

Pentlow Drive, once the railway goods yard, has a wild plum hedge between it and the main road together with mixed native trees.

In the 1960s houses were built at the Columbines and here and at later developments, areas were assigned for ornamental trees and shrubs.

The new gardens along the main road have a wealth of new trees including paper bark maple, red oak, golden beech, dawn redwood and cedar Atlantica Glauca. Although hidden and insignificant now, an aerial photograph in years to come will show a different picture.

Poplar trees along the old railway embankment
Rosemary Freeth

Corsican pine in Cavendish churchyard
Rosemary Freeth

FLORA & FAUNA

Lime tree on Cavendish Green
Rosemary Freeth

One of the old elms in the hedge from Embleton House
Rosemary Freeth

Survey of Cavendish Churchyard - 16 April 2001 and 16 July 2001

Ash	Avens, wood
Barley, wall	Beech
Bent, creeping	Bindweed, field
Bindweed, large	Bittercress, hairy
Bittersweet	Box
Bramble	Brome, barren
Brome, false	Bryony, white
Burdock, lesser	Burnet-saxifrage
Buttercup, bulbous	Buttercup, creeping
Butterfly bush	Campion, bladder
Cat's-ear	Celandine, lesser
Cherry, wild	Chestnut, horse
Chickweed, common	Cinquefoil, creeping
Cleavers	Clover, red
Clover, white	Cocksfoot
Cowslip	Cranesbill, doves-foot
Creeping Jenny	Daisy
Daisy, ox-eye	Dandelion
Dead nettle, white	Dock, broad leaved
Dock, wood	Dog-violet, early
Elder	Elm
Fennel	Fern-grass
Fescue, red	Forget-me-not, field
Foxglove	Golden rod, Canadian
Ground elder	Ground Ivy
Groundsel	Hawksbeard, beaked
Hawksbeard, smooth	Hawthorn
Herb Robert	Hogweed
Holly	Honeysuckle
Horehound, black	Ivy
Knotgrass	Lilac
Lime, common	Lords and ladies
Mallow, common	Meadow grass, annual
Meadow grass, rough	Medick, black
Michaelmas daisy, common	Mouse-ear, common
Mustard, garlic	Mustard, hedge
Nettle, stinging	Nipplewort
Oak, pedunculate	Oat-grass, false
Ox-tongue, bristly	Parsley, cow
Parsley, fool's	Pearlwort, procumbent
Periwinkle	Pine, Corsican
Pineappleweed	Pink-sorrel

Plantain, greater
Plantain, ribwort
Primrose
Ragwort, common
Sandwort, thyme-leaved
Shepherds purse
Sow thistle, perennial
Speedwell, germander
Speedwell, thyme-leaved
Spurge, petty
Strawberry, wild
Thistle, creeping
Timothy grass
Wall-rue
Willowherb, greater
Woundwort, hedge

Plantain, hoary
Poppy, opium
Privet
Rye-grass, perennial
Self heal
Sorrel, common
Sow thistle, smooth
Speedwell, ivy leaved
Speedwell, wall
Stonecrop, biting
Teasel, wild
Thistle, spear
Violet, sweet
Willowherb, American
Wood-rush, field
Yarrow

Survey of the Cemetery, Cavendish - 16 April 2001 and 16 July 2001

Agrimony
Barley, wall
Bedstraw, ladies
Bent, creeping
Bindweed, large
Birds-foot-trefoil
Bittersweet
Bramble
Bryony, white
Burnet-saxifrage
Buttercup, creeping
Cats-ear
Cinquefoil, creeping
Clover, red
Cocksfoot
Cranesbill, cut-leaved
Cranesbill, hedgerow
Daffodil
Daisy, ox-eye
Dead-nettle, red
Dock, broad-leaved
Dog-rose
Dogwood
Elm, small leaved
Field-speedwell, green

Aspen
Bedstraw, hedge
Beech
Bindweed, field
Birch, silver
Bittercress, hairy
Blackthorn
Brome, barren
Bugle
Buttercup, bulbous
Buttercup, meadow
Chickweed, common
Cleavers
Clover, white
Cowslip
Cranesbill, doves-foot
Cypress, Leyland
Daisy
Dandelion
Dead-nettle, white
Dock, wood
Dog-violet, early
Elder
Fescue, red
Forget-me-not, field

- Fumitory
- Ground elder
- Groundsel
- Hawksbeard, beaked
- Hawthorn
- Holly
- Horehound, black
- Knapweed, common
- Lords and ladies
- Maple, field
- Meadow-grass, rough
- Medick, black
- Mouse-ear, common
- Oat-grass, false
- Periwinkle, greater
- Plantain, hoary
- Poplar Lombardy
- Ragwort, common
- Rye-grass, perennial
- Selfheal
- Snow-in-summer
- Sow-thistle, perennial
- Sow-thistle, smooth
- Speedwell, ivy-leaved
- St John's wort, perforate
- Stonecrop, reflexed
- Strawberry, wild
- Thistle, spear
- Violet, sweet
- Willowherb, American
- Willowherb, rosebay
- Woundwort, hedge
- Yew
- Grape-hyacinth
- Ground ivy
- Hawkbit, lesser
- Hawksbeard, smooth
- Herb Robert
- Honeysuckle
- Ivy
- Laurel
- Mallow, common
- Maple, red
- Meadow-grass, annual
- Mouse-ear hawkweed
- Nettle, stinging
- Parsley, cow
- Plantain, greater
- Plantain, ribwort
- Primrose
- Rowan
- Sandwort, thyme-leaved
- Snowdrop
- Sorrel, common
- Sow-thistle, prickly
- Speedwell, germander
- Speedwell, thyme-leaved
- Stonecrop. biting
- Stonecrop, white
- Thistle, creeping
- Timothy grass
- Wellingtonia
- Willowherb, hoary
- Wood-rush, field
- Yarrow
- Yorkshire fog

Surveys in this chapter were conducted by Ron Hartley and members of the Sudbury and District group of the Suffolk Wildlife Trust

Cavendish family coat of arms featured on the village sign

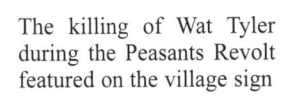

The killing of Wat Tyler during the Peasants Revolt featured on the village sign

63

BUILDINGS THROUGH THE VILLAGE

Cavendish contains many attractive houses from the 15th century or earlier to the present day. Amongst them are 75 listed buildings, 21 of which are thatched.

The dating of property is always an inexact science since documentary evidence of alterations is rarely available, and owners were often keen to adopt the latest style. Many more recent facades conceal older structures behind. Earlier domestic houses were built without chimneys and these were added later when other changes took place. The local abundant supply of oak provided materials for timber framing which was in-filled with wattle and daub or lath and plaster.

By starting at the Clare end of the village it is possible to 'travel' through this chapter and to learn more about some of the properties and the people who lived in them. The owners of the houses have contributed to the accounts.

Cavendish Hall

Cavendish Hall is set back off the main road from Clare. The entrance to the long drive up to the house is flanked by two lodges. The house is believed to have been built by Thomas Halifax, once Mayor of Chester for one of his sons. A heraldic window in one of the rooms shows the date 1802. A catalogue from H Philip of Bond Street dated 17th November 1814 announces a seven day sale to be held on the premises, of the entire contents of the house, including 300 dozen bottles of 'old port', the property of Captain Ogden deceased. Two prints (from the same plate) show the house and garden, one entitled 'Cavendish Hall - the seat of Sir Digby Mackworth Bart' and the other 'seat of Dr Yelloly'. The Yelloly family continued to own the Hall until the death in the 1930's of the last Dr Yelloly and the house was then sold to the then sitting tenant, Mrs Brocklebank. Mr T S Matthews, husband of the present owner, purchased the house from Mrs Brocklebank in 1969.

Yew Tree House, built originally as a farmhouse around 1420, was at the time part of the Cavendish Hall Estate. On old maps it can be found named 'Kings Farm', 'Yew Tree Cottages' and 'Wayside' eventually returning to the present name in the 1970s. 'Further Street' was the address. Between 1806 and 1850 the house was part of the Cavendish and Warren Estates.

Yew Tree House

The oldest deeds are dated 1898 when the house was owned by Samuel de Beauvoir Yelloly (retired Royal Navy officer) and the Rev S T Fisher of Borley Rectory.

1911	Jointly owned with the Rev H F Bull of Borley Rectory
1938	Sold by the Yelloly family to Miss Fanny Hughes Mortlock for £150, one side only being habitable. The house remained in the Mortlock Family until 1970.
1966	Miss Hilda Mortlock received a grant of £275 13s 3d from Clare Rural District Council to add a bathroom.
1970	sold to Mr Cave who restored the house from the two cottages to one property.
1972	sold to Mr & Mrs Dickson
1975	Bought by John and Margaret Kurtz who continue to live there.

Moone House was originally built as a farm cottage in the late 18th century, and has a timber frame. It was called Ward's, presumably after the tenant who lived there.

At some time during the 20th century the cottage was converted into a public house, called The Fir Trees. The sign hung above the front door, (now blocked off) and the bar was situated in what is now the sitting room. The landlord provided an additional service and many people can still remember how it was possible to buy a pint of beer at one end of the room and have a haircut at the other.

Moone House

The house was extended to provide a 'cellar'. This was above ground as there were no foundations, let alone a basement. Deliveries were brought in through the back yard which is now the drive. There is now a vigorous wisteria growing by the front entrance. This used to be the back door and a grape vine grew there. Children used to eat the grapes whilst waiting for their fathers to finish their beer and come home.

In 1965 the pub was no longer viable since the farm workers who used to drink there had long since been replaced by machinery. The house was sold, subject to a covenant that it could never again be used as a pub, and changed hands three times in twelve years. Local builders (and undertakers), Fitch and Mitchell, who operated from the barn next door, helped to extend the house further including the creation of a good sized dining room.

Prior to 1977 the house was owned by two Irish brothers, who changed the name from the Fir Trees to Moone House. The bus company, however, continued to refer to the unmarked stop as 'The Firs'.

Cavendish Mill is situated at the end of Mill Lane which is the road on the right after Moone House. There is a reference to a mill in Cavendish in the 1086 Domesday Survey, but its exact location then is not known. A water mill at Cavendish called Paddokes Mill was mentioned in documents in 1463. George Offord was the miller at a Patrick Mill in 1855 and the deeds of the property show it to have been in the occupation of the Offord family between 1828 and 1945. In 1767 a Daniel Offord was deemed to be one of the principal inhabitants of the parish when he became a co-signatory of an agreement between the parish and the couple looking after those suffering from smallpox in Overhall or 'Pockey Hall'.

Cavendish Mill

The Mill was used as a water mill to grind corn and was eventually demolished between the wars, probably during the 1920's. When building work was being undertaken in recent years it was discovered that the rubble from the mill had been used to backfill the sluice. After the Offords left the house was owned by a number of families and for a period of time in the early 1970's was run as a restaurant.

The oldest part of **The Red House** (at the eastern end) was built in about 1500. It is thought that as the owner prospered, further additions were built on, with the increase in his status and wealth being reflected by more and more ornate carving on the beams at each stage.

At the western end of the property is the present dining room, built about 1530, which contains very heavily carved timber beams. The running oak leaf design mirrors that on timber outside under the gable. (The workhouse manager is said to have lived in this part of the house. The workhouse used to be across the road in the house now known as Layfield.)

The Red House

The house was at one time known as Four Cottages and the road it is on used to be called Workhouse Street. The late Arthur Deeks, born 1902, spoke to the present owners about some of the people he remembered living in each. In the western end in number 1 at the rear facing Clare lived a Mr and Mrs Wordley with their 3 sons and 2 daughters. He worked on the land and although 'very poor were a good and honest family'. In number 2 lived Mr and Mrs Ben Richardson with their 3 or 4 sons and 1 daughter. The sons moved to London to work as porters on the railway. Mr Richardson was head linesman on the railway and later moved to the Gate House at the Mill Road crossing. Mr Beeton and a Miss Beeton lived at number 3. Arthur Deeks went to school with him and Mr Beeton became a Flight Lieutenant in the Second World War. Mr and Mrs Jim Turp lived at number 4. He had a club foot and in spite of this used to push a handcart around Cavendish and Pentlow selling bloaters.

The house was once part of the Cavendish Hall Estate and the couple who lived next door, Charles and Hilda Finch were employed to work as butler and chambermaid for the Brocklebanks at Cavendish Hall.

The present owners bought most of the property in 1985 and after buying the easternmost part in 1987 converted it into one home from where they provide Bed and Breakfast accommodation.

Layfield appears to date from the early/mid 16th century and was probably a village farmhouse. It had a small hall parallel to the street with two small service rooms at the west end with a chamber above. At the east end a parlour wing projected forwards to the street also with a chamber above which was jettied out at the front. In the 17th century a large room was added to the main range at the west end and a fireplace constructed in the hall. In about 1790 the house became the village workhouse. Records describe the conversion work to the house and provide an inventory for each room.

Layfield

Green End is known to have been occupied in the early 17th century and may have even earlier origins. The property was sold in February 1613 for the sum of £33 'lawful money'. During the 18th century records show that it was sold or leased to a number of people of differing trades or professions including wool comber, husbandman, yeoman, blacksmith and shopkeeper.

Green End

It is known that the house was divided into two if not three properties and in 1839 a granary was erected at the rear by the gentleman living there, a wool comber. In the same year he took out a fire policy through the Independent and West Middlesex Insurance Company as he was in the business of singeing worsted.

In 1861 it was bought by Thomas Walter Waring a gentleman who had a barn built at the rear and the house fronted in white bricks. His initials and the names of Samuel Viall of Colts Hall, Ambrose Smith of Nether Hall as well as presumably the men who worked on it, Jacob Rice, glazier and Robert Page, cabinetmaker are carved on the bricks high up on the front of the house to the left of the front door.

The house became known as Rose Villa and Thomas Waring later became a surgeon. The family who moved there in 1953 named it Green End after the village in Hertfordshire from whence they came.

The Greys

The Greys stands overlooking the Green. Part of it is built at a slightly lower level, demonstrated by the difference in roofline. It is thought that this half could have been added later to house an increasingly wealthy family. The upper part was built in the 16th century and then in 1769 was given a gothic 'makeover' when arched windows and rendered panels were added concealing the timber framing underneath. This date is carved high in the rendered wall of the south gable end and seems to reflect both internal and external changes made at this time. A small wing was built onto the back of the Greys to house the striking 17th century staircase. The panelling on the walls in the sitting room and the panelled doors also date from 1769. An early merchant mark on an oak lintel provides some evidence as to the house's early history.

Virginia House & Any Lengths Hair Care

Across the road from Green End stands **Virginia House** and its adjoining shop premises. It is thought to have been built in about 1490 as an open hall house with ceiling and chimney stack added about a hundred years later. Some of the timbers are smoke blackened and there is evidence that there may have been a smoke hood. In 1790 the property was sold to Richard Ambrose a farmer and butcher. It stayed in the Ambrose family until 1908 when it was sold to Frank Hale. It later passed to his son Joe and was sold to another butcher in 1981. In 1986 the building was still on well water and had no mains drainage. Mains supplies were connected in 1987.

There used to be much land attached to the property, between the old and new river towards Pentlow where the cattle used to graze. Sheep would graze on the green. Over the years many strips of land were sold off leaving only about 2½ acres now. At the rear was the slaughterhouse and from the church tower one can still see the track across the green taken by generations of animals.

In the mid 1980's the shop ceased to be a butcher's and became Cavendish Tea Rooms. It was then a video shop and later a computer supply and repair shop. In 1992 it was opened as **Any Lengths Hair Care**. The shop still retains the old corner payment kiosk from the butcher's days. Under the front canopy are the original game hooks on which now hang many hanging baskets which are enjoyed by the entire village.

BUILDINGS THROUGH THE VILLAGE

The Grape Vine is believed to date from about 1518. During the latter part of the 19th century the house was a 'Dame School', run by the Misses Clark. One of the pupils in the 1890's was Tom Ambrose (Basil's father). The Misses Woodward ran the property as The Tudor Guest House for many years. Their brochure tells that Cavendish 'is on the Eastern Region railway line from Liverpool Street' via Marks Tey and also that at night, 'the Cavendish Cinema provides good entertainment'.

The Grape Vine

In the 1960's the house became a restaurant and was renamed The Grape Vine. The present owners ran the restaurant from 1975 until it closed in 1986 and the house reverted to domestic use.

The building next door was for many years the home of the village blacksmith, George Barltrop. Behind the house was the forge with its fire fanned by large bellows. It was here that he shoed the horses, made and repaired tools and machinery. After his death the premises were sold to the Reverend J D Barnard, as a home for his retirement. Sadly he spent little time there as he had a tragic accident when he fell through an open trap door and later died. The Sue Ryder foundation then purchased the property which is now used as a **shop** by the charity.

Sue Ryder shop

Manor Cottages are believed to date from the 15th century, originally built as one property they are now three houses. In the westernmost cottage there is a plasterwork coat of arms in the downstairs ceiling. In heraldic terms the shield is a combination of Cavendish with Smith and presumably refers to the marriage of John Smith of Padbrook House, Cavendish and Joane, daughter of Sir Thomas Cavendish in 1478. In the easternmost cottage there is a similar coat of arms over the fireplace. At the beginning of the 20th century the building was used as the Manor House School for young ladies and was run by the Misses Larkin. It later became the Reading Rooms and Recreational Institute. Newspapers and books were available here and there was also a billiard table downstairs.

Manor Cottages

A school was founded on the site of **The Old Grammar School** in 1696 by the Reverend Thomas Grey, Rector of the Parish, although parts of the front of the house date from the 15th century. Further major building work was completed in

1749 and this date is recorded on the chimneystack on the front northwest corner of the property. Other additions were made to the building and the school operated until 1907.

After the school closed the property became a private residence and in 1935 two thirds of the front elevation was demolished to make way for the building of a cinema.

During the early 1980's the front rooms of The Old Grammar School were used as 'Tea Rooms'. The attic at the front of the house has been reconverted into a bedroom. When the school was open it was in part a boarding school and the attic was used as a dormitory. As it was owned by the same family who ran Pentlow Hall Farm, the food for the school came from there.

Debenhams, Old Cinema & Old Grammar School,

Garth Cox lived with his mother and sister at The Old Grammar School and it was he who decided to build a private **cinema** in place of part of their home. A newspaper report at the time stated 'It was felt that Cavendish and the surrounding villages were in need of facilities for popular cinema entertainment'. The article encouraged people to support the venture and congratulated the proprietors (Garth and his sister) on their enterprise. The builders were T Martin & Sons of Clare and an opinion expressed at the time was that the cinema 'although of modern design, blends harmoniously with the picturesque aspect of the village'. The re-upholstered seats came from the Royalty Theatre, London. The cinema boasted seating for over 200, central heating and the 'Nesthill Bantam Bucket hand pump system' to guard against fire. It had special ventilating apparatus, acoustic plaster and the latest lighting and Philips Cine Sonor projection and sound equipment in addition to a neon sign.

The first programmes included 'Wonder Bar' starring Al Jolson and later in the week 'Danny Boy'. Other showings included 'Hound of the Baskervilles' and all the programmes being screened in the local main towns. The Coronation of Queen Elizabeth II was also shown. The cinema was closed in 1956.

In 1960 Cavendish Lingerie Company opened the building and remained on the site for nearly 10 years. The building is now used as a store for Sue Ryder Care.

Debenhams originates from the 15/16th centuries with later additions. It is constructed of oak and elm studwork retaining some wattle and daub infill under outside rendering in the older parts. There have been two more modern additions – one around 1900 and a new kitchen was added about 10 years ago. There are two large brick chimneys, one with a restored inglenook fireplace. The house was originally thatched but is now tiled after some restoration in about 1978.

It is thought that the house was possibly a servant's house to the then adjoining Grammar School as it has a large, previously ruined washhouse at the back, where possibly school clothes could have been washed. It is now an artist's studio.

At one time the house was lived in by a Mrs Smith around 1912. An elderly man once called at the house and asked to look at the house as he remembered visiting his grandmother there. There used to be an outside privy at the back and an open well in the garden. Another resident of the house was a Miss Grace Goodie – a relation of W G Grace the cricketer.

It was once a butcher's cum 'sweetie' shop (for the 1930's cinema built near by) and was owned in the 1930's by a Mr Debenham who had a wooden leg. He was known in the village as 'Skimps' Debenham because he was reputed to be apt to give short measure.

The house was known as 'Bretts' at one time and also as 'Kyrenia' when it was owned by a Cypriot, who surprisingly the present owners knew when they worked in Cyprus.

Previously there was a thatched house on the site of **Melford House** and in 1897 the present house was built around the thatched property and the very large central chimney was retained. This newer house was built as a shop with a baker's oven incorporated into the building at the rear. Next to Melford House, on the west side, was a small 'two up, two down' cottage with stairs winding around a central chimney. This was demolished in 1955.

Melford House

Hyde Park Corner Cottages, famous the world over, were built in the 16th century. They gained their name when house guests at the rectory who were up from London, would harangue the locals here, and the name stuck.

By 1954 the five cottages were in a dilapidated state and under threat of demolition. Tom Ambrose could not countenance such a loss to the village. He, along with other residents decided to try and save them. They set up the Cavendish Preservation Society and bought the cottages. Sir Alfred Munnings agreed to be president of the Society. In his autobiography he wrote, 'I know of no better group than these thatched, lime washed cottages at the top of the Green, clustered around the church'. They received encouragement from the Suffolk

Preservation Society, West Suffolk County Council, Clare Rural District Council, Historic Buildings Council, The Pilgrim Trust and the Society for the Protection of Ancient Buildings. An appeal was launched and money for restoration raised. Bill Rice of Cavendish was the builder who undertook the renovation work and a thatcher from Norfolk was employed.

Hyde Park Corner Cottages

The restored cottages were handed over to the George Savage Trust to provide homes for elderly and needy people of Cavendish. They were opened by the Earl of Euston in 1958.

On 12th April 1971 the cottages were severely damaged in a fire. Firemen spent nearly nine hours at the scene. Although the cottages were insured there was a shortfall of £8000 for the rebuilding work; however people gave generously. The cottages were rebuilt by Bailey and Goates Ltd and the thatching was done by Frank Linnett. For this work he won the 1972 cup for the 'Best Reed Thatched Properties' presented by the Suffolk Master Thatchers' Association. The cottages were re-opened by the Duke of Grafton in 1972.

Chinnerys was built during the 16th century and over the years has seen some additions and changes of use. At the turn of the last century in 1900 it was run as a butcher's shop by the Chinnery family and during the 1950's was a garage with petrol pumps outside. In 1975 it became an antique shop, which it remains to this day and has even featured on the cover of a brochure in Japan. Another claim to fame is the old Victorian post box inset into the building – not for public use.

Chinnerys

Middle Cottage and Tumbleweed (previously Waver View) were built as one hall house no later than 1450 and possibly earlier. It was home to a well to do man, probably a yeoman and his family. There was no fireplace and smoke from the chimney went through the eaves of Tumbleweed. Evidence of this smoke is still visible on the roof timbers. The walls were constructed of wattle and daub and some still exists. There are exposed beams which demonstrate the presence of a high table (later adopted by Oxbridge Colleges to seat their dons) placed above floor level and of a canopy over the high table both of which were to escape

BUILDINGS THROUGH THE VILLAGE

draughts. There were shutters in place to help control the draught before windows had glass. A solar, or upper chamber, was added about a hundred years later. This now forms part of Spring View, the third cottage in the row. Also in the 1500's the chimney and fireplace were added.

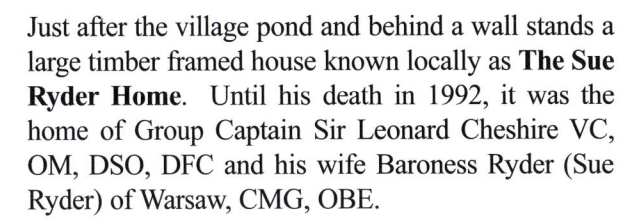

Middle Cottage & Tumbleweed

Just after the village pond and behind a wall stands a large timber framed house known locally as **The Sue Ryder Home**. Until his death in 1992, it was the home of Group Captain Sir Leonard Cheshire VC, OM, DSO, DFC and his wife Baroness Ryder (Sue Ryder) of Warsaw, CMG, OBE.

It was built in the 16th century and a document dated 1577 states it to be the rectory at that time. It was home to the Reverend Thomas Castley between 1808 and 1860. It was sold in 1860 to Joseph Stammers Garrett, who the following year sold it to Edward Fisher who then sold it back to Joseph in 1871. It subsequently accommodated many people including the minister of the Congregational Church which was built by Mr Garrett.

Sue Ryder Home

In 1920 it was the home of Mr & Mrs Frances Shepherd. Mr Shepherd had the first radio loudspeaker in Cavendish. On a Sunday evening a popular treat was for anyone to go into the front garden to hear the service being broadcast from St Martin in the Fields church in London.

The wife of Major General Neville White bought the house in 1926. After his death she married Mr William Mortimer. He was later killed in an air raid and his widow stayed in the house until it was sold to the Ryder family in 1946.

After her war experiences, Sue Ryder established the foundation in 1952 to stand as a living memorial to the victims of war and those who suffer from racial intolerance. The nursing home was set up to create a home for survivors of the Nazi concentration camps. In 1953 the Old Rectory became the headquarters for the Sue Ryder Foundation. Over the years more accommodation was built in the grounds to provide long term, respite and palliative care for the residents. A gift shop, restaurant and museum telling the story of Lady Ryder's life and work were created. There is a chapel at the home used by Anglicans and Catholics and services are held there. These are attended by the residents and local Christians of different denominations.

On reaching the age of 75 Sue Ryder gave up her role as a foundation trustee and agreed to become the organisation's figurehead. The name was changed to Sue Ryder Care and two years later in November 2000 Sue Ryder died. The administrative staff were moved from Cavendish and in September 2001 an announcement was made regarding the planned closure of the home at Cavendish before the end of the year.

The Dower House is mentioned in a terrier (i.e. Register) of glebe or church lands by the Rev. Thomas Grey, Rector of Cavendish in 1686.

'In primis the Rectory House with the Orchyard, garden, barns, stables Dower House and other edifices belonging in the possession of the present Rector aforesaid.'

The Dower House

His 'Rectory House' is now the old part of the Sue Ryder Home, still known to many villagers as 'The Old Rectory', because it *was* the rectory for 300 years or more down to 1860.

The cottage now called 'The Dower House', in the High Street, originally stood between the Rectory and the road. But in 1808 the formidable Thomas Castley became rector and remained so until his death in 1860. He disliked the way the cottage obstructed his view, and other people's view of his house, so he had it moved to its present site in 1825. He kept a remarkably detailed log of his many activities, quarrels, alterations to the church and the Rectory, and so on, but few of them seems to have made him prouder than having shifted this little house. He returns to the subject frequently in his log.

1871	Shown on a plan of The Old Rectory Estate as divided into two dwellings.
25/9/1871	Sold by Joseph Stammers Garrett, Corn Miller, Merchant, Maltster and Farmer of Blacklands, Cavendish to John Cockerton, Beer shop keeper of 'The Fir Trees', Cavendish for £125.
10/8/1884	Inherited by John William Clarry, Cheesemonger (Provision Merchant) of 154, Green Street, Bethnal Green, Middlesex.
17/2/1913	Death of J W Clarry in Cavendish.
13/2/1916	Death of Mrs Maria Jessie Clarry in Cavendish. Inherited by Walter Joseph Clarry and his sister Mrs Jessie Sarah Prince.
21/11/1917	Bought by George Richardson of Cavendish, Beer House Keeper for £80.
6/1/1931	Bought by Herbert Mortlock, Builder for Cavendish for £65.
8/10/1945	Bought by Mrs Florence Amelia Savage of Brick House, Hartest, Suffolk for £800.

BUILDINGS THROUGH THE VILLAGE

24/12/1964	Bought by W B Kingsbury and Sons, builders of Commerce house, Boxford, Suffolk, for £4,500.
1982	Restoration and extension.
29/6/1983	Bought by Terence Saville, Civil Engineer and Marion Saville of Epping Upland, Essex.

The Post Office was built as a timber framed farmhouse in the 17th or 18th century. The outside was clad in brick during the Victorian era and the house extended.

It was a butchers shop in the 1920's run by a Mr Prentice and a covenant exists forbidding the present owners to sell meat or meat products or slaughter animals on the premises. It became the village Post Office in the 1940s.

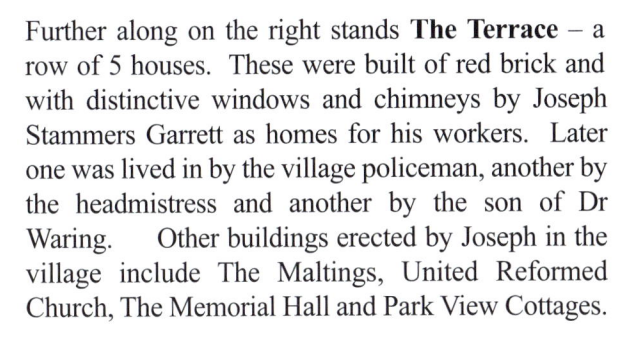

The Post Office

Further along on the right stands **The Terrace** – a row of 5 houses. These were built of red brick and with distinctive windows and chimneys by Joseph Stammers Garrett as homes for his workers. Later one was lived in by the village policeman, another by the headmistress and another by the son of Dr Waring. Other buildings erected by Joseph in the village include The Maltings, United Reformed Church, The Memorial Hall and Park View Cottages.

The Terrace

Iona was built in the late 17th century and the copyhold tenant in 1776 was a William Hammond. Upon his death in 1793, the Lord of the Manor of Overhall and Nether Hall, Thomas Ruggles Esq. granted copyhold to his nephew, a village carpenter. The property was then described as a 'messuage or tenement, together with the houses, outhouses, yards, garden and orchards'.

In 1822 the copyhold was eventually passed to Micah Mellor, a confectioner who after financial difficulties was declared bankrupt in 1853. The property was put up for sale in three lots by public auction and the copyhold secured by William Orbell, the younger, of Pentlow, a farmer. On 17th December 1855, William died and left his estate (of which Iona was only a part) to his wife Catherine

Iona

75

'provided she should so long continue his widow, she keeping the same in good and tenantable repair and condition and committing no waste therein'.

On Catherine's death twenty years later, the estate was sold by auction on 16th June 1876. The messuage (lot 5) went to William Chatters, a maltster's labourer. In 1922 William Chatters purchased the freehold from the Lord and Lady of the manor of Overhall and Nether Hall – John Samuel de Beauvoir Yelloly and his sister Elizabeth Sarah Rosalind Yelloly for £24. Three days later on 21st December the ownership passed to Mrs Clara Banks the wife of William Banks (a butcher). The central cottage was at this time occupied by Mrs Ellen Amelia Mansfield who ran a sweet shop there. She purchased the three freehold cottages in 1925.

Mrs Mansfield gifted the property to her son Sidney in 1937, a Sergeant in the RAF. On 17th July 1945, Sidney, now a Flight Lieutenant sold it to Mr Jack Clark and his wife Kathleen. For the whole of their occupancy until 1982 the cottage had no indoor sanitation or water – the toilet was at the bottom of the garden. The electricity supply was taken out at their request because of the accident to Mr Wells in the village pond.

In 1982 Mrs Clarke moved into a nursing home and after renovation the house, now a single residence came to the present owner.

The Old Post Office

Believed to date back to the 15th century, **The Old Post Office**, with its thatched roof, is typical of many cottages in the village. The smoke blackened timbers in the ceilings of the upper rooms in the central part of the building are representative of a single storey, single room dwelling, of that part of the medieval period, which would have had an open fire in the centre of the floor and a hole in the centre of the thatch to enable the smoke to escape. Now on two floors, there is a Tudor brick fireplace at the west end of the building. The bricks in the fireplace were cemented together using a lime mortar and the mixture and its constituent horsehair is still visible.

The Tithe map of 1848 and corresponding ledger, documents the building as being owned by Joseph Stammers Garrett. To the rear of the property was a building which is shown as being a Maltings. The house called 'Palings' now stands on the site of the old Maltings. During recent excavations two bricks were found bearing the initials JSG, originating from the brick kiln works which was on the bottom road to Glemsford and also owned by Joseph Stammers Garrett.

By the beginning of the 20th century photographs show the building as a Post Office and it remained as such until the 1940's. It is known that the building fell into a state of disrepair until the early 1970's when a local thatcher bought the property and was largely responsible for restoring it for use as a family home.

Western House was the site of an old hall house. It was rebuilt in about 1670 and was made into two houses over the years and then reverted to one dwelling. It was named Western House because it was a staging post on the Western Stagecoach run from Norwich to Bristol. Horses would be changed here and passengers could stretch their legs and have refreshment.

Western House

In 1735 it was owned by Thomas Revell a grocer and in 1799 the house and cottages were owned by Joseph Burroughs, a shopkeeper and his wife Alice. After other owners it was bought for £400 in 1831 by William Henry Colt, a draper and then in 1878 was sold to Joseph Byford a carrier.

In 1901 it was sold to Henrietta Garrett who lived there until her death in 1944. During this period she ran a very small and select school which Mrs Matthews from Cavendish Hall can remember attending. Western House changed hands a further four times before being bought by the Marshall family in 1970. Since then it has provided the base for the Full of Beans wholefood shop and for singing and music lessons.

Originally Western House had about five acres of land with three gardeners. In 1912 the garden area between Western House and Granby Cottage was the site of a dwelling house, bakery, grocers and post office. There were several cottages and tenements in Ram Alley with many tenants over the years including in 1736 one James Bond.

Along the High Street, near the bend stand **Peacocks** and **Melcott House**. They were originally built as a single house. It is a good example of a medieval hall house and one of the older properties in Cavendish, having recently been dated, on inspection of various architectural detail, to between 1470 and 1480. The house was most likely built as the project of an up and coming wool merchant. The middle section of the house, until recently simply known as Melcott, was the hall of the house, where dinners and entertainments would have been hosted. The western end of the building, which is a separate property named Peacocks, was the kitchen and pantry.

Peacocks & Melcott House

77

There has been some effort to peer into the recorded history of the property, which seems to have been subdivided into separate houses for many years. The earliest ordnance survey maps seem to indicate at one time it may have formed six dwellings. The internal fabric of the house would seem to suggest that the basic structural subdivision into three separate properties has been in place for perhaps two or three hundred years.

Until the 20th century there stood in what is now the garden of the properties a horsehair matting factory. The actual factory building seems to have occupied the entire space that was the garden of Beehive Cottage, beginning where the present garage stands and projecting back to where the allotments are now. In evidence of this is the property that stands to the rear of the building known as Factory Yard Cottage. No doubt the presence of industry in the vicinity explains why, at the height of its operation, the building which is now Melcott House and Peacocks was home to so many families.

Chippins

Further along on the left hand side of the road past Water Lane stands a thatched cottage known as **Chippins**. It was given this name by the previous owner who was a Master Joiner. Chippins was built in about 1450 as an open hall house. It had a large central hall open to the roof where the smoke from the fire in the hearth drifted through. At the lower end of the hall was a buttery and pantry with sleeping quarters above and at the other end was a doorway to a room with solar above which was used as a private area for the yeoman owner. There is a crown post roof upstairs and it is this which the owner could look up at when he sat at his raised dais bench and table at the upper end of the hall. Behind him and on the wall above were arch braces and these timbers can still be seen today as can the slots in the timber where the dais bench fitted.

In other parts of the building carpenters marks can be seen which show how the house was originally assembled. Taper burns exist where the timbers were singed from the lighting. Before glass was commonly used, the house had wooden shutters and the peg holes and parts of the the outer frame for these are still visible in places.

In the 16th century the hall was floored over and a central chimney added and in about 1570 the gabled end of the building was built on. It is thought that, as there is no evidence of an original external door here, this was like a granny annexe, since the widow of the previous owner could not inherit and the house would pass to her son.

Over the years owners have included John Christmas, a yeoman and Henry Symonds a cordwainer who made high quality shoes out of fine leather.

In recent years the house was divided into three dwellings- the central one occupied at one time by the retired stationmaster. In the late 1970s it became two properties and work is currently being completed to turn it back into one dwelling as it was over 500 years ago.

Blue Monk Cottage was built in the 16th century. It was formerly three cottages and at one time was the site of the builder's yard and undertakers run by Mr Page.

Today it is the site of Cavendish Arts shop selling rattan furniture and baskets from around the world.

The **Memorial Hall** or Lecture Hall, as it was long called, was built by Mr Joseph Stammers Garrett of Blacklands Hall in about 1870 and was given to the Congregational Church in Cavendish and vested in trustees in 1902.

Blue Monk Cottage

It was designed as a day and Sunday School and as a centre of educational and recreational activities for the benefit of the people of Cavendish. The dwindling number of children in the parish led to its disuse as a school. The building was requisitioned by the military during the 1939 - 45 war, and was used by the Highland Light Infantry.

The Charity Commissioners granted permission for it to be sold and it was advertised for sale by auction on 18th April 1946. The late Mr & Mrs Harold Ince of Station House thought that the building would make a good village hall and at a public meeting on 6th April 1946 Mr Tom Ambrose agreed to lead negotiations to purchase the hall. The hall was purchased for £466 before the auction.

The Memorial Hall

On 17th May 1946 Lady Gordon Finlayson suggested in a meeting that the hall should be renamed The Memorial Hall in token of the Victory and Peace Celebrations. A Management Committee was formed, grants were obtained and major alterations were undertaken in the early 1950's including the addition of a stage and dressing rooms. The late Mr and Mrs Harold Ince and the late Donald Bain QC were very keen on amateur dramatics.

In 1955 the toilets and entrance hall were built and in 1977 the Jubilee Room was added. Today the Memorial Hall and Jubilee Room provide a focus and venue for many of the village activities including the Pre-school Playgroup, Horticultural Society, Women's Institute, badminton and other meetings.

Station House was originally a house with Victorian origins and two cottages. It is situated on Pentlow Lane, alongside the former Sudbury to Cambridge railway line. The line closed in 1967 and there are still remains of the shallow railway embankment along part of the meadow. The house was owned by William Churchyard, a retired brewer, who in 1855 worked at the White Horse. He died in 1878 and left the property and adjoining cottages to his niece Ann Coe. The house and one cottage were eventually bought by Harold Ince in 1925 and in 1930 he acquired the second cottage.

Station House

Harold Ince owned a gentlemen's outfitters in Clare (where today Peddars men's clothes shop stands). He and his wife were very active in village life and were keen that the old Lecture Hall, later Blacklands School, should be given a new lease of life as a village hall. They helped to set up the dramatic society and debating society. Mrs Ince was a member of the WI and WVS and was a great organiser.

In 1973 Dr le Masurier bought Station House and later some land on the north bank of the River Stour where he used to graze his sheep. The present owners bought the property in 1997.

Down Water Lane towards Glemsford stands a large imposing building set back from the road. This is **Blacklands Hall**, one of the farms in the village. Blacklands is referred to in one of the directories of the 19th century as a very ancient structure. It is thought to have been built about 1480 although it could have been earlier since some speak of links with Sir John Cavendish. The house has undergone many changes and additions over the years.

Blacklands

There is a cottage, named Kimsings, adjoining the property at the western end and it is in the west wing of the hall that the oldest part of the building, with lower ceilings, can be found. The house is heavily timbered and the central area was probably part of a hall house.

When work was being undertaken recently on the largest central chimney, evidence of a fireplace was uncovered about half way up, indicative of a previous floor at that level where none exists today. Over the front door is a carving indicating that the house was restored in 1576.

There is no clear history of ownership but references can be found to different owners and tenants over the years. Between 1785 and 1797 there is a record of an agreement for payment by John Ambrose. In 1844 it was owned by John Ruggles Brise of Spains Hall, Finchingfield and in the occupation of James Heckford.

In September of that year there was a fire in a hayloft at Blacklands. The local paper reported that James Heckford was very grateful for all the help he had received from all. He is said to have declared 'the poor have misconducted themselves in many parts of the country but there are some that know and will do their duty when required'.

Between 1845 and 1850 Blacklands was extensively remodelled by the Ruggles-Brise family and the eastern wing was added.

Joseph Stammers Garrett bought Blacklands Hall Estate in 1853 and lived there until his death in 1899.

It has been in the ownership of the present family since 1900.

Cavendish C.E.V.C.P. School 2000

Bentley Photographic

SCHOOLING – THEN AND NOW

Cavendish has been blessed with schools of various types and at one time there were six schools in existence, including two 'Dame Schools' and the Sunday School. The buildings which housed these schools still exist, but only the Voluntary Controlled Primary School remains.

The schools were founded because of the social, religious, academic and political convictions of their founders, and the progress and problems of education in the Cavendish schools are well documented in log books and minute books kept by the head teachers and managers. National and local events and their impact on the community also figure in these records.

1. The Voluntary Controlled previously known as the National School or the Church School or the Top School.
2. The British School also known as the Congregational School, or the Blacklands School or The Bottom School.
3. The Sunday School based at the Church.
4. The Grammar school. The remaining part of the building is a private house named 'The Old Grammar School' which faces on to the village green.
5. The Private school run by Henrietta Garrett. This was at Western House in Lower Street (now High Street).
6. The Private School run by the Misses Sarah and Martha Clarke. This was at the house now known as 'The Grape Vine', which faces the village green.

The Grammar School

Cavendish Grammar School was founded by the Reverend Thomas Grey, Rector of Cavendish in 1696. The buildings for the school were provided by him and its income through the rental of a house and shop in Cavendish and a farm of 78 acres in Pentlow.

The rules for the government of Cavendish Charity and School laid down by him were very lengthy and detailed.

The Master was:

> 'from time to time to teach children in the said school for ever, in the English, Latin and Greek tongues
> to keep the said school and school house and other houses in good and sufficient repair
> to be bound and obliged to go to prayers with the children in the said school every morning and every evening'.

War Memorial & Grammar School

Details of the required readings and teachings were then given with the instruction that the Master and children should:

> 'come to the Parish Church every Sunday and Holy Day; and for the neglect of any of these things, such Master to be displaced'.

Some of the other provisions included the assistance of promising lads to be apprenticed to a trade, or to be prepared for entry to Cambridge University. Poor children of Cavendish whose parents did not pay poor rate were to be taught for free. Those parents who did pay poor rates were to come to terms about fees with the schoolmasters.

In spite of fluctuating fortunes, in 1863 the Grammar School was re-established by the Charity Commissioners as a classical School for 30 boarders. The school continued until 1907 when it was wound up and the premises sold. From then on the endowment provided scholarships from the local elementary school. The farm was sold in 1938. Part of the school building remains now called 'The Old Grammar School'. The rest of it was demolished to make way for a privately owned cinema.

The National School

Cavendish National School, sometimes known as the Church School or the Top School and now known as the Voluntary Controlled School is a first school for children aged 5 to 9 years. In 1863 – 1864 the National or Church School at the top of the village green cost £817-13s-6d to build. It was reckoned to accommodate up to 200 pupils and that its annual expenses would be £70. These were to be found by school fees of 2s 6d ($12\frac{1}{2}$p) for first child in the family and 1d for following children. In addition there were to be collections in church, subscriptions and government grants. During the first few years the average attendance was 78. By 1905 the paying element had gone and attendance was compulsory for all children up to 13 years of age with certain exemptions. The school was under the control of the state and a logbook was kept by the headmaster.

The following facts are recorded in 1905:-

>The schoolroom $54\frac{3}{4}$ ft long, 18 ft wide, 11ft high - 98 pupils.
>The class room $24\frac{1}{2}$ ft long, $16\frac{1}{3}$ft wide, 11 ft high - 40 pupils.
>The infants room $26\frac{1}{4}$ft long, 15 ft wide, 11 ft high - 39 pupils.

>Total 177 pupils

There was a staff of three assisted by monitors, monitresses and a pupil teacher.

The log book continues to give a fascinating picture of the struggle to educate so many children of such a wide age range in such limited quarters and reports show that excellent results were obtained. In addition it shows a most interesting picture of the social history of the village and increasing interest in the health and welfare of the children.

The continuing dominance of the church is shown by the Diocesan Inspector's report of 1906, which includes frequent use of the word excellent, and ends, 'but might not more attention be paid throughout the school to bowing the head at the name of Jesus'.

1905	Headmaster – Mr Hutchinson with two assistants.	
	Correspondent	Mr Hugh Clark.
	Managers	J Offord
		R W Waring

The National School – 1920

Sept 18th	Average attendance 149.9 = 98.5%
Oct 2nd	Received a list of moral lessons and cigarette smoking.
Oct 25th	Note by Correspondent 'Infant room overcrowded – 57 children including 18 under 5 in accommodation for 45'.
Nov 5th	Extract from Government Report – 'The school maintains its excellent character'.
Dec 4th	3 Absent through nasty eruptions on the faces.

1906
Jan 18th	School closed – polling station for General Election.
Feb 6th	Mr Hindle took names of 8 children who wish to sit for Labour Certificate and 1 for age exemption.
Feb 28th	8 children sent to British School for Labour Exam.
March 14th	Received result of Labour Exam – all 8 passed and entitled to leave school (at age 11 if a job is available).
March 23rd	One child left today – labour certificate.
June 8th	School closed for 1 week – the Fair.
Sept 25th	School closed to take party of scholars to the Zoological Gardens in London (Cavendish had a railway).

1907
Feb 28th   Labour Exam held at British school – 3 passes, I failure.
Sept 23rd   Commenced school – harvest not finished.
Nov 21st   Gardening classes started for 14 boys.

1908
Apr 28th   School closed due to the outbreak of Diphtheria.
Apr 30th   School re-opened after disinfection of the school.
Sept 14th   School commenced, 128 present 99% attendance.
Dec 3rd   School closed till January 4th due to Scarlet Fever.

1909   Government report spoke very highly of school's academic achievement and discipline.

1910
Aug 3rd   Doctor took the Maypole and Morris Dancers to Clare.
Dec 6th   3/- of faggots received (to light school fires)

1911
May 23rd   More fever in Workhouse Street (now Stour Street).
Sept 13th   Choir outing to Clacton.
Dec 5th   Case of Poliomyelitis.

1913
Jan 9th   Weighing machine received from Stoke. Weighed and measured all children.
Jan 10th   Weighing machine sent to Blacklands School.
Mar 19th   His Grace Archbishop of Melbourne visited the School.

1914   No reference in Log Book to the declaration of war.

1915
Feb 1st   Patriotic concert for Belgian Refugee Fund.
Mar 23rd   4 children sent home by Dr Courtauld suffering from mumps. Much whooping cough in school.

1916
May 22nd   Clocks put back 1 hour.
Sept 23rd   Due to late harvest school remained closed until Oct 2nd.

1919
Apr 1st   Gladys Bettinson appointed as monitress.
July 18th   School closed for peace celebration.
July 11th   Cyril Harris won scholarship to Sudbury Grammar School.

Sept 13th   Cookery class commenced for – Winifred Brown, Sybil Long, F Underwood, R Banks, D Pettinson, J Foster, M Rosebrook, E Cooper, M Plumb and M Pryke.
Nov 1st   Attendance low due to sickness caused by shortage of water in the wells.

The National School cricket team – 1923

1921
Mar 18th   Attendance 99.5%
July   J Banks won scholarship to Sudbury Grammar School. H D'eath won Grey's scholarship.

1923
Jan 25th   Week of heavy rain and floods. Children's eyesight tested.

1924
June 27th   75 pupils went on visit to London Zoo.
Nov 4th   Dr McCullough extracted teeth of children aged 5, 6 and 7.

1925   First intelligence testing of children.

1926
Jun 11th   Admitted 4 children from the fair.
Sept 24th   Assyrian Patriarch visited the school.

1927
Jun 30th   Several children absent – gone to Clacton with Sunday school outing.
Sept 5th   School opened. Admitted 23 children from the Blacklands School which has been closed.

1929
Jun 19th   12 boys to attend woodwork classes at Glemsford on Tuesday afternoons.

The British School

This was sometimes known as the Congregational School or the Blacklands School, or the Bottom School. When the National or Church School was built in 1863 – 1864 there were objections in Cavendish (as there were in many town and villages) to the religious teaching of the Church of England being imposed on all children. The result was the founding of the British School at the other end of the village – largely led by the Stammers/Garrett family at Blacklands Hall. There had been a 'dissenting rag school' in Cavendish prior to this, but the present Memorial Hall was in fact the British School, the hall being the main teaching room and the smaller room the infants teaching room. The school eventually came under the authority of the West Suffolk County Council and on July 6th 1903 there was a Managers meeting to form a properly comprised body of managers when the following were present: -

>   Rev D L Jones
>   Miss Garrett
>   Miss O J Thompson
>   E Graham
>   Mr S J Garrett

At this meeting the following appointments were made: -

>   Chairman   -   Rev D L Jones
>   Correspondent -   Miss Garrett
>   Foundation Manager - Mr S J Garrett

Throughout its existence managers met at various places: -

>   The Old Rectory (home of Miss Garrett)
>   The Steam Mill
>   The Maltings Office
>   The Lecture Hall (main part of school)
>   The vestry of the Congregational Church

Again the Minute Book of the managers gives a picture of the progress and events in Cavendish, and indeed the school's struggle for existence.

1904	Head Master's salary - £100
	Assistant Teacher's salary £45/£50 if appropriately qualified.
	Pupil Teacher £8 per year to teach 20 hours per week.
	Headmaster criticised for administering severe corporal punishment, which led to many complaints from parents.
	An ambulance class started in the Lecture Hall.

1905   Requisitions for the School cost: -

Needlework	£2 7s 8½d
Stationery	£1 1s 9¼d
Books	£2 19s 0d
Apparatus	7s 8½d
Kindergarten	£1 6s 4¼d
Total	£8 2s 6 d

1906
Feb 22nd   Name of the school changed to Blacklands School.
The headmaster Mr Castle was present at a meeting to answer questions and the following resolutions were passed: -

1. No boxing on the ears.
2. No corporal punishment till the end of the session.
3. Punishment to be in strict proportion to the offences.
4. Any further signs of vindictiveness will not be overlooked by the Managers.

May 10th   (Not surprisingly) Mr Castle resigned, having been appointed headmaster of Princes Risborough British School.

1907   The headmaster, Mr Graham, was asked not to make applications for holidays for football and was informed that the Managers would only grant holidays for 'sensible reasons'.

Salaries

Mr Graham	£110 0s 0d
Asst Mistress	£ 57 8s 0d
Asst Teacher	£ 34 0s 0d
Monitress	£ 7 10s 0d

School closed in December because of Scarlet Fever.

1909 A report of the school stated: -
The school is well staffed and general progress is quite satisfactory. A new timetable is needed, as the afternoon arithmetic is not required. New caretaker appointed at £9 per annum and this to include the provision of all cleaning materials.

1910 Roll: Mixed 126 Infants 29

Letter from West Suffolk County Council stating that the condition of the toilets was totally unacceptable. The managers comment was that there were no funds for 'the offices' and help would be sought from all and sundry.

Letter from West Suffolk County Council: -

'owing to the smaller number of children, notice to be given to Mr Graham and Miss Evans that their service would not be required after Feb 28th. The school for the future to be carried on by a headmistress and a supplementary teacher.'

1913	Two monitresses were -	Elsie Maylon
		Ethel Brown
1915	Two monitresses -	Hilda Prentice
		Olive Petit

Suggested by the West Suffolk County Council the school be closed during the war.

1921 West Suffolk County Council made suggestions for a new scheme for schools.

1925 Further letters concerning the condition of the school and its closure. The Managers were clearly against this but –

1927
Aug 31st School Closed
Books and furniture removed by an Education Officer from Bury St Edmunds.

The children were transferred to the National School, which records admitting 23 of them on September 5th 1927.

Private Schools

These were sometimes called Dame Schools or Academies, and are known to have existed in Cavendish. The house called the Grape Vine was such a school run by the Misses Sarah and Martha Clark. Miss Henrietta Garrett ran another at Western House but it is unlikely that the number of pupils exceeded 10. Both of these schools were closed during the first half of the 20th century. A directory of 1844 also lists academies run by Mary Ambrose and Susanna Jay.

Cavendish CEVCP School – Schooling Today

The Cavendish school as we know it today caters for children aged 4 to 9 years, after which they transfer to Clare Middle School. Children attend the school from Cavendish and also Glemsford, Clare and other villages in Suffolk or Essex. At present there are 68 pupils on the roll with a steady upward trend.

Misses Sarah & Martha Clark proprietors of the Dame School (now The Grape Vine)

Today most pupils wear sensible and attractive uniforms and the Cavendish schoolchildren are dressed in red and grey. The school elected to become Voluntary Controlled but keeps a close connection with the village church and holds a monthly service there.

The school has strong community links which Mrs Gillian Garrett-Moore the present Head is keen to promote. The Cavendish pre-school group is encouraged to visit the school thus easing the transition from one daily activity to another. Visitors from the village are encouraged to attend concerts, church services and to come into school to meet with the children. Other regular visitors include teachers from liaison schools, Clare Middle School, the Police, the Education Welfare Officer who checks children's attendance, photographers and many others. Health visits are made by the dentist and nurse.

SCHOOLING - Then and Now

Outside visits include theatre workshops, the zoo, museums, local shops and 2 day camps. After school events include swimming, football and indoor table top games. The local Brownie pack meets at the school. The swimming pool was originally built during the early 1970's instigated by the then head, Mr David Burbridge. The labour was provided by parents and other village organisations. The Community Council helped with the fundraising. The pool is used during holiday periods for the benefit of the school families.

The village green is used by the school for games and sports. It also offers an excellent opportunity for geography and environmental studies. Extra land behind the school was acquired seven years ago and to celebrate the millennium the children planted 250 trees there.

The school day follows the National Curriculum, with early years pupils attending part-time. Pupils 5 to 7 years study Key Stage 1 and those aged 8 and 9 years follow Key Stage 2. The same subjects are covered in both Key Stages

Maypole dancing on the village green *Denise Davies*

concentrating on english, mathematics and science. Amongst other subjects included are information technology and religious education. Statutory Assessments Tests (SATS) are set at the end of year 2 and other curriculum tests are also taken. School dinners are provided from Clare or children take a packed lunch. As part of their physical education pupils perform country dancing, and the tradition of dancing round the maypole has been revived.

After leaving the school, children attending Clare Middle School conduct a village study during the summer holiday after year 7. Some of these village projects have been in great detail. Parents very often become involved, resulting in the children having a greater awareness of the village where they and in some cases their grandparents have lived.

Reminiscences of School Days

Tom Ambrose

Tom Ambrose of Nether Hall, born in 1890, attended the Miss Clarke's School and the grammar school where he was Head Boy in 1904. Tom told his son;

> 'Morning break was held at a different time from the National School so that pupils did not come together on the village green.'

Millicent Buckle

'I went to live in Cavendish in June 1911 when I was five. The teacher was a Miss Brown. The flat, black hat with a big black ribbon bow, black skirt and blouse she wore I'll always remember. She was a strict and fine teacher. I owe much of my handwriting skills to her. We didn't use script. About five or six of us little girls sat on a long bench.

One day, I imagine her lesson must have been about steam, because she put the question, 'What was the water in the steam engine for?' Silence prevailed and then this little girl put up her hand. I'll always remember her black mop of curly black hair, her round rosy cheeked face and she replied: 'To make a cup of tea'. We all burst out laughing heartily. Miss Brown didn't think it so funny and came down the row of us boxing our ears and banging our heads together.'

Ellen Corner (Nee Grimwood)

'My family moved into Cavendish in 1953, when I was eight, and so I went straight into Miss Willis' junior class (at this time there were three classes: infants, juniors and, for those who didn't make it through the 11 plus, the seniors, a class of 11 – 15 year olds). Miss Willis was bright and breezy and encouraged us with her winning smile. Her class was at the back of the school and it housed along one wall the County Lending Library books. It was here I discovered and rapidly read my way through P G Wodehouse's Jeeves and Wooster books.

Having missed out on time in the infant class with the cuddly and kind Miss Gladys Bettinson, it always seemed to me that this was the best class in the school. It was a sunny room, with colourful posters and all the interesting paraphernalia of craftwork and learning through play, which was distinctly lacking in the rest of the school. We made brief forays into her class for the weaving of multi-coloured, quirkily shaped raffia mats.

However, onwards, and possibly, upwards. With the opening of the secondary school in Clare which scooped up the 11 – 15 year olds, us older juniors were propelled into the scary atmosphere of Mrs Cowey's 'top class'.

There was that cheery chap on the BBC school radio singing programme, who enthused us to sing along with him 'The Vicar of Bray', and 'Sweet Lass of Richmond Hill' (my children read this in amazement - these were the high points?). Oh yes, and the privilege and liberation of being sent to clean and dust Mrs Cowey's schoolhouse – and polish her brassware. The tasks were irrelevant, and, in my case, probably not very well performed. We were out of the classroom – hurray! The boys had an even better time, so I thought, tending the vegetable patch. This might account for the lack of brassware in my own house, and the great attraction I've always felt towards vegetable gardening. There was no school playground as such, but we had the run of the green at break times, (somewhat alarming the butcher's flock of sheep who quietly grazed there), and tremendous 'grass fights' when the long grass of the green was cut for hay in the early summer. Then there were the lovely student teachers; I think they must have come on the train from Cambridge, to do their teaching practice at Cavendish. We loved them! They seemed so glamorous and sophisticated in their full-skirted flowery dresses and high heels. I recall their last day with us, as they struggled off down the road with arms full of huge bunches of home-grown flowers, our thank-you for being just so exotic and wonderful.'

St Mary's Church, Cavendish

CHURCHES

St Mary's Church

For 700 years St Mary's, more or less in its present form, has been a landmark, but there are indications that the site has been a centre for worship for much longer. For instance, we know that 'Edric the Deacon' went to the Battle of Hastings but unfortunately failed to return.

About 1300 the Normans began the transformation of the Anglo Saxon church (probably wooden) by building the tower from local flints. In 1381, during the Peasants Revolt, the rebels captured and executed the local magnate, Sir John Cavendish. The church benefited however since Sir John left sufficient money in his will to rebuild the chancel.

The next time that national events impinged on the church (apart from a possible visit by Elizabeth I) was during the Commonwealth, when a certain William Dowsing led a team of wreckers through East Anglia, destroying what he termed 'graven images'. This led to the smashing of the stained glass windows and the mutilation of the font. William Dowsing would hate to know it but he inadvertently did the church a good turn, since it is flooded by light coming through the plain replacement glass.

In the 19th century the chancel ceiling was boarded and decorated, an organ was installed and a vestry built and more recently some pews have been cleared away to allow greater freedom of movement.

The church has survived a good many changes and is still here to give its silent witness.

The following is a summary of some of the many changes which the church has undergone over the centuries.

About 1300   the tower, the porch and the lower part of the north and south aisle walls were built. The 14th century door has a sanctuary ring on the outside. The chimney shaft in the tower is part of the original building. A room in the tower was built to be lived in (presumably by the rector) with a fireplace and a window giving a view of the high altar.

About 1350	the south aisle walls were raised to their present height and new windows and buttresses added.
About 1383	the chancel was built through a bequest by Sir John Cavendish, Chief Justice of the Kings Bench, who was beheaded in 1381 during the Peasant's Revolt. He left the sum of £40 for the building of the chancel on condition that the work began within 12 months of the Easter following his death. The chancel is at a lower level than the nave and is one of only four churches in the country where this is the case.
About 1425	the north aisle was rebuilt with new windows inserted. Over the north door and elsewhere in the walls, Roman bricks (possibly from a local villa) can be seen.
About 1485	the nave arcade and clerestory were built possibly by the same masons who worked on Long Melford Church. An inscription (much of it illegible), along the top of the windows outside, records that this part of the church was erected by the Smith family, who intermarried with the Cavendish family in the 15th and 16th centuries.
1570	The tomb of Sir George Colt was built in the sanctuary.
1862	Organ chamber and choir vestry built.
1987	The bell turret was blown down in the October hurricane.
1989	The bell turret was restored.

In 1553 five **bells** were recorded, which possibly gave rise to the name for the 'Five Bells' public house which is nearby. None of these original bells remain. In 1779 William Mears of the Whitechapel Bell Foundry cast a ring of six bells. His son Thomas joined the business in 1787 and he cast the roof bell in 1797. Two of the six bells are from the 1779 casting, the tenor has been recast twice and the others were recast in 1930, by John Taylor and Co. of Loughborough at the same time as a new bell frame was installed.

The timber structure housing the roof bell and weather vane was blown down in the great gale of October 1987 and it was replaced in 1989. The roof bell has never had a clapper fitted, presumably to prevent it from striking in the wind.

The other six bells have interesting inscriptions which, with their original inscriptions, are reproduced here;-

Treble Bell 4 cwt -	'I MEAN TO MAKE IT UNDERSTOOD ALLTHOUGH I'M LITTLE YET I'M GOOD' MEARS LONDON FECIT 1779
Second Bell 5cwt -	'IF YOU HAVE A JUDICIOUS EAR YOU'L OWN MY VOICE IS SWEET AND CLEAR' MEARS LONDON FECIT 1779 RECAST 1930
Third Bell 6 cwt -	'MUSICK IS MEDICINE TO THE MIND' MEARS LONDON FECIT 1779
Fourth Bell 7cwt -	'PEACE AND GOOD NEIGHBOURHOOD' MEARS LONDON FECIT 1779 RECAST 1930
Fifth Bell 8 cwt -	'OUR VOICES SHALL IN CONSORT RING IN HONOUR BOTH TO GOD AND KING' MEARS LONDON FECIT 1779 RECAST 1930
Tenor Bell 11 cwt -	CAST BY JOHN WARNER AND SONS LONDON 1869 'THE GIFT OF AMBROSE SMITH ESQ NETHER HALL CAVENDISH W DOWNS OF MELFORD HUNG ME'

There is only one bell ringer based in Cavendish now and should a peal be required for a wedding, the support of volunteers from another village is required.

Four of the bells (1 2 3 6) are used for the chiming of the clock with the tenor (6) also being used to strike the hour.

The **clock** has two plates on which are inscribed:-

> 'This clock
> was given to the PARISH of
> CAVENDISH by the pious
> Bounty of Matilda the
> Wife of Ambrose Smith
> Yeoman of Nether Hall in
> The same PARISH in the
> Year of our LORD 1871'

> Made by W DOWNS & SON
> Long Melford
> Suffolk
> 1871

It is said that many years ago the owner of a farm near the former Glemsford Rectory was out in his fields when he was enveloped in a dense fog and completely lost his bearings. After wandering about for some time he became increasingly distressed and anxious. To his great relief he heard the clock at Cavendish strike and from this was able to reorientate himself and find his way home. The farm was renamed Clock House Farm and in his gratitude he made an annual payment to the church wardens of St Mary's Church, Cavendish.

The clock used to require winding every other day, but now it has an electrical winding mechanism. This has reduced volunteer input considerably although attention is still required after power cuts and when we move our clocks backward or forward in autumn and spring.

In the early 1960s the clock was renovated and the face was regilded by Bill Rice and John Pratt. Bill's daughter, Carol Gladstone was only young at the time. She can remember the clock face in their dining room - 'it looked enormous'.

The **organ** was installed in 1838 and before that a pitch pipe was used. The organ is said to have come from a big house in Luton. The present organist Rodney Bullock was asked to provide temporary cover and is still playing 35 years later.

It is thought that Cavendish has always had a church **choir.** At present it has a membership of 12 ladies, although over the years all ages and both sexes have been represented. In 1999 the choir lost its longest serving member when Don Angel died. He had sung in the choir for 84 years until 2 weeks before his death. The choirmaster is Peter Leigh and each year, he and the choir take part in the Diocesan Choir Festival. From time to time they also sing at Clare, the only other church in the Stour Valley Group to have a choir.

The **churchyard** has 249 burial plots with records between 1689 and 1886 although there is a site for the internment of ashes.

The first entry for the **cemetery** dates from 1887. Many of Cavendish's former residents are buried here including Group Captain Sir Leonard Cheshire VC, OM, DSO, DFC and his wife Baroness Ryder of Warsaw CMG, OBE, and founder of the Sue Ryder Homes. Many headstones bear Polish names indicative of those who came to the first Sue Ryder home - in Cavendish - as 'forgotten friends of the Allies'. One of the more striking memorials in the cemetery is

St Mary's Church choir – late 1940s

that of an angel. It marks the grave of Beatrice Cordell who died aged 23 as a result of an illness on 6th July 1923. Just a month earlier, as Beatrice Brewster, she had married in the church. Her father, who owned the stores in Cavendish, paid for the erection of the **Lych Gate** to the cemetery. On the main beam facing the entrance are the words 'In Memoriam' and on the inside beam is the inscription, 'To the glory of God and in loving memory of the wife and daughter of H J Brewster whose bodies rest nearby. This lych gate was erected August 1939'.

The War Memorial stands on the village green in front of the church and cottages. It was designed with a deliberate gothic feel so that it would blend with the church when viewed from afar. The green, on which the Memorial stands, is in a conservation area with many listed buildings surrounding it. The War Memorial itself was granted Grade II listed status during 2001.

The architect was Leonard Crowfoot of Long Melford and it is thought to be his only War Memorial Commission in Suffolk, possibly he was chosen as he had done some work on the Church School in 1912.

Lych gate to the cemetery

The Memorial was unveiled and dedicated on 19th September 1920 by Col. Sir Courtney Warner Bt., CB, MP, Lord Lieutenant of Suffolk. In 1923 fence posts and railings were erected around it to protect it from the cattle that grazed on the green. It was renovated and in 1948 the World War II names were added. A further name was added after the Cyprus 1956 conflict. It is very unusual in Suffolk for a Memorial to contain the names from three conflicts and there are thought to be only 7 others.

1914 – 1918

Otto Adams
Stephen Henry Argent
William Ballard
Victor W Bullock
Sidney Basil Clarry
Osborne Hale
Charles Neville Hutchinson
Richard Johnson
Frank Johnson
Harry Maxim
Jas Wm Parmenter
William H Parmenter
Walter A Skeemer
Albert Steff
Arthur Wells
Frederick Wells
William John Wordley

Geo W Argent
John Ballard
John F Brown
Hugh Cuthbert Clark
Fred Fitch
Trafalgar Percy Hartley
Claude E S Ince
Jack Johnson
Arthur King
William Maxim
Samuel Alderson Parmenter
Robert Savage
Charles Slater
Frank William Underwood
Edward Wells
Charles A Wordley

1939 - 1945

Peter Andrews　　　　Victor Brown
Reginald C French　　Eleanor Johnson
Cyril A Taylor　　　　William Tharby

Cyprus 1956

William R Doe

Cavendish is unusual in having had at least four **rectories**. It is even suggested that the room with a chimney in the church tower served as a home for one of the earliest rectors. From Tudor times until 1862 the rectory was based in the house, set back and east of the pond, known as the Sue Ryder Home. A new rectory was then built in the grounds of Overhall where it remained until 1947. A house called the Yews, next to Cavendish House and opposite the pond was then purchased and this continued as the home for the rector. This is now called The Old Rectory! During the early 1970's a new development of houses was built, forming Grey's Close. A property here then became the next rectory until the Stour Valley Group of Parishes was formed in 1986 and the rector's base moved to Clare.

In the 18th century the Church was keen to promote literacy along with religious education and Sunday Schools were founded for these purposes. Cavendish **Sunday School** was formally started in 1787 and was staffed by well meaning people who undoubtedly taught many of the more able pupils to read.

A note in the rector's log of 1844 refers to the great day of celebrations for the 57th anniversary of the Sunday School.

A further note in 1864 refers to a meeting of the Sunday School teachers at the new rectory when twelve attended. Tea and cakes were provided before the meeting with a memo that in future 'ale must be had in addition to tea'.

The average attendance at this time was 82 boys and 54 girls.

Just over 100 years later in 1967 there were 3 classes with approximately 30 children. The Sunday School met in the church before the morning service and were not involved in the actual service. Other activities included outings by train or bus to the seaside, and a Christmas party in the school or Memorial Hall.

By the mid 1980's numbers had greatly declined as a result of other organised

Sunday school outing 1907

activities on a Sunday morning. The Sunday School closed in 1990 when there were less than 10 pupils attending, all less than 10 years of age.

United Reformed Church

Before the present building was erected in 1858, the local Congregationalists used to walk to Clare to attend the chapel there. Joseph Stammers Garrett, a maltster, miller and corn merchant was a staunch non-conformist and was a member of the chapel committee at Clare. He built the Congregational Chapel (now United Reformed Church) in his home village of Cavendish. His daughter, Henrietta Garrett was a very active member of the church for 75 years until her death in 1944, being organist for 55 years and treasurer of chapel funds for 26 years.

In 1906 the interior of the chapel was renovated with a new floor and ceiling and repairs to the roof. Electric light was installed in the church in 1932 and further internal decoration and external repairs were carried out in 1937. The Women's Bright Hour came into being in 1935 and continued to provide an opportunity for regular meeting together until the 1980's.

United Reformed Church

PUBLIC SERVICES

Health

When the Romans laid the road which is now the A1092, they elected to follow the Stour River valley rather than search for higher ground, which they usually preferred. The Saxon settlement which became Cavendish was therefore situated in a very wet swampy area, prone to flood and not likely to favour the health of its inhabitants. Certainly plague, ague (malaria) and other fevers were prevalent in East Anglia in the Middle Ages, together with leprosy, small pox, cholera, typhoid and diseases related to contaminated water supply, unsanitary housing conditions and poor diet. Of all these, plague was certainly the most devastating. History records the worst ever epidemic was in 543 AD, when parts of the British Isles were almost depopulated, and the last major outbreak in England in 1665/6 resulted in 'one third of the population in many towns being swept away, and in East Anglia two thirds of the clergy fell at the post of duty'. Even in 1910, ten cases of the plague were reported over the border in Essex, causing the Medical Officer of Health to order intensive rat hunts to destroy the fleas that transmitted the disease.

A newspaper article about Cavendish in 1859 stated 'The health of this village is anything but good; the situation being low on the ground is muddy and damp. In the past few weeks several people have fallen victim to consumption, and many children ill with pains in the chest, legs and head' (possibly rheumatic fever). It continues 'It is questionable whether our forefathers acted wisely in selecting swamps and marshes such as Cavendish for their habitation, for even now flood water enters the houses and roads'. The last significant flooding of houses in the village was in 1969, and has since been avoided by better drainage systems.

When the Domesday Survey was published in 1086, Suffolk had a relatively high population of 70,000 people (equivalent to 40 per square mile) and Cavendish was reported to be 'wealthy'. The poverty and riots of the 14th and 15th centuries, combined with the 'Black Death' of 1348 which eliminated half the population, caused a steady decline in both health and the economy, later halted in Suffolk by the prospering wool trade. When this too declined in the 16th and 17th centuries various laws were passed in the 1660s to boost the national income, one requiring woollen shrouds to be compulsory for all burials, and another raising taxes by charging two shillings a year for every hearth in each house. This caused much hardship in poor rural areas, as agricultural incomes were very low. In 1601 a Poor Law Act had made each parish responsible for funding the care of the sick, aged and unemployed, and much charitable help was given by the church and local gentry. No medical care was available for the general population, other than simple home remedies and the advice of 'wise women' or witches, travelling charlatans and quacks. Probably more victims were poisoned than cured!

Pockey Hall – copy of drawing by Miss Sarah Clarke 1861

One of the earliest records of organised health care in Cavendish relates to 'Pockey Hall', a part of the original Overhall building, which was reserved for smallpox victims. In 1767 an agreement was made between churchwardens and parishioners and Samuel Nutman and his wife, to provide meat, drink, beds and all necessities for the inmates. They were to nurse and wash them, and repair all window glazing, for a salary of 33 shillings a year. The parish would provide medicines, petticoats and clothing, and make an allowance for dependants of victims. Those that died from the disease were to be buried at night by law. Smallpox itself was gradually controlled by Jenner's discovery of vaccination, and this was made compulsory in 1853. The disease now appears to have been eradicated worldwide. Sadly little remains of 'Pockey Hall'.

In 1758 a 'physician and surgeon', Richard Hawes, must have been living in this area, as he was appointed Medical Attendant to the Parish Workhouse, a building on the north side of Stour Street, now known as Layfield. His salary was to be 6 guineas a year, out of which he had to provide all necessary medicines for the inmates. The Governor or 'overseer' was obliged to supervise the work done; the baking of bread and cooking, brewing of ale and 'keeping of pigs'. He was to ensure the inmates were 'clean and decent'; fires were allowed only in the same room as the sick. Arrangements were to be made for the washerwoman and 'layers out' of bodies to have an allowance of one quart of ale. (This was then the staple drink, which is just as well as the water quality was very questionable!) In 1834 a Poor Law Amendment Act closed all the village workhouses, and groups of parishes (42 in this part of Suffolk) combined to form 'The Union' – a large central establishment situated in Sudbury and now the Walnut Tree Hospital. Here there were separate wings for men and women, children, the mentally retarded, mothers of illegitimate babies, vagrants and tramps.

During the 19th century many advances were made in the provision of better living conditions and health care, though rural areas became relatively depopulated owing to the massive exodus to the growing towns during the Industrial Revolution. Scientific advances and medical knowledge had surged ahead, and in 1860 doctors were required to be properly qualified by the Royal Colleges of Physicians and Surgeons. Apothecaries, quacks and the wise women and 'Mrs Gamps' who had been the forerunners of nurses and midwives, were replaced by properly trained doctors and nurses. Not before time perhaps: a local newspaper report of April 1860 records how a small child in Cavendish drank water from a kettle on the hob, and was rushed to the 'wise woman' next door, who 'blessed' it and wiped her finger three times round the mouth. All this was to no avail, as the child died the next day from the scalding, the inquest being held at the George Hotel.

The remains of Pockey Hall today *Denise Davies*

Many of the news items at this time relate to farm accidents, fires or deaths due to falls from buildings, ricks or wagons. Drunken brawls were not uncommon often involving fights with lads from nearby villages. Infant and child mortality were high; outbreaks of infections such as measles, polio, scarlet fever, diphtheria and TB were frequent and often fatal; as there were no known treatments. Cattle diseases were rife and with no trained vets, farmers relied on the traditional stockman's remedies; dairy farms in particular were a source of infected milk, leading to bovine TB in children. This, together with rickets and polio, resulted in a high incidence of bone and joint disease in children, and many were crippled.

Into this medical minefield in 1844 a Dr Thomas Waring set up in practice as the first 'GP' in Cavendish. He served a large area, covering many miles in his horse and trap to visit the sick and deliver the babies. A very ill patient might need two or three visits a day; puerperal fever was still a danger after confinement, and there were very few effective treatments available; one had to 'watch and wait'. Daily morning surgeries were held (including Sundays), but not evening surgeries; and a request for an emergency visit would be made by a neighbour fetching the doctor in person. As antisepsis improved, and anaesthetics such as ether or chloroform became more widely used, minor surgery could be carried out either at the surgery or in the patient's house, only very serious accidents being sent to hospitals in Sudbury or Bury St Edmunds. Dispensing was done by the doctor, making up medicines, pills and ointments, for which the patient had to pay unless very poor; and visits at home or to the surgery were subject to fees, forming the bulk of the doctor's income. A lot of midnight oil was no doubt burned in 'keeping up the books'; the doctor's wife would be secretary, receptionist and possibly even dispenser! The doctor was also responsible for paying a fee to the District Nurse or Midwife until their status was improved and they were properly registered by their own governing bodies.

In 1906 Dr A L Ritchie joined Dr Waring's son Richard in partnership. Dr Ritchie's son Ted has written a fascinating account of his father's practice in Cavendish until 1942. He says that his father found the village 'quiet, self-sufficient and very 'East Anglian'' when he first arrived; he stayed, bought a house, with meadow, a horse and trap, and his share of the practice, all for £900. In 1909 the doctor acquired his first car, and was said still to be the only car owner in the village even in 1920 (and the High Street had not yet been tarred!). In 1916 a move was made to Blacklands, which became the family home as well as the practice premises. Patients would queue outside before morning surgery, and apparently complained that the waiting room was bare, cold and uncomfortable. Private patients were seen by appointment in the family dining room and lighting was provided by gas made from petrol on the premises!

As the practice grew, and more villages such as Alpheton, Cockfield, Long Melford, Liston and Foxearth were covered, Dr Ritchie took a partner, and built a new residence and surgery at Embleton House in 1932. By this time a lady dispenser was employed and Nurse Goodchild was the District Nurse in the village.

Dr A L Ritchie on his mare Starlight at Rose Villa c. 1913

Dr Ritchie died in 1942 and was followed by a succession of family Doctors (Dr Crowther, Dr Stevens and then Dr O'Brien) who are fondly remembered by a few of today's older residents. In 1950 after the start of the National Health Service, the surgery was moved to 2 Park Cottages, patients from Glemsford attending there until their own branch surgery was built in 1965. By 1970 the population of Glemsford had increased so much it was decided to build a new central surgery there and Cavendish then functioned as a 'branch'. Three GPs now use the central surgery to provide a fully comprehensive and up to date service, with ancillary staff, nurse attachments, dispensing and all modern facilities including computers. Other practices in Clare and Long Melford will also accept Cavendish patients on request.

Many years of planning and reform preceded the start of the National Health Service in 1948. In the 1880's, County, District and Rural District Councils were established, with responsibility for public health, sanitation, water supplies and sewage in their own areas. Rural services in particular improved, wells, springs and streams were checked for pollution, cesspools removed from gardens and replaced by pails and outdoor toilets. Once an adequate water supply had been achieved (at the expense of the parish!), main sewers were laid in the village during the 1950s; but some wells and outside toilets remained in use for much longer. The first Ministry of Health was formed in 1919; infant mortality and death rates had declined considerably in the previous thirty years; children were healthier, but birth rates had fallen slightly. The School Medical and Nursing services were started in 1918 and continued until the 1939 - 45 War; and in the Cavendish School Log Book entries illustrate the changes in childhood illnesses: -

In 1908 Diphtheria and Scarlet Fever
    1911 Polio
    1913 Weighed and measured children
    1915 Mumps and Whooping Cough
    1919 Gastroenteritis (there was a drought, the wells dried up and the water supply contaminated).
    1923 Eyes tested
    1924 Dr McCullough extracted teeth
    1941 Dental inspection and extractions

Many of these illnesses have been almost eradicated by food hygiene and effective infant immunisation.

On the welfare side the elderly and poor people had benefited greatly from the introduction of the Old Age Pension in 1906; the National Insurance Act of 1911 (Lloyd George); the provision of better hospital services, home nursing and midwifery, and above all, proper housing and diet for most. Nevertheless, rural areas still suffered, in the 1920s and 30s, with a marked downturn in work and population, which continued until the Second World War. Children and babies were then given extra vitamins and free school milk, and clinics provided for regular checks and advice to young mothers. The 'NHS', however, was needed to pull all the services together, but the speed of medical advances and techniques since the war have quite outstripped the available funds. One consultant wrote, 'The cost of the NHS was not correctly forecast, and it was grossly underestimated. If it had been known beforehand, no politician would have had the courage to vote for the Bill'. To the public, especially the less well off, it was a blessing – they could consult the doctor, but would not get his bill!

Fitness and life expectancy have increased remarkably in the last 100 years, and the 'quality of life' is the criterion now used to judge the success of medical care. The causes of death are no longer mainly epidemics and infections but are more related to ageing disorders, and to the stresses and strains of modern life. The health of Cavendish folk should benefit from living in a village which was described by a passing visitor years ago as 'sweet and lovely, where all is peace and sunshine'. If not, should we blame the Romans? That swampy ground is no longer a hazard, but their road certainly is!

Law and Order

At a town meeting in Cavendish in 1768 thirteen villagers passed the following resolution:-

> 'Whereas frequent robberies are committed upon those present by persons unknown, we are determined to prosecute such as shall hereafter be detected and convicted of any such felonies at our joint expense. We are further determined that such as shall be convicted shall be excluded from all benefits or collections that may arise in the parish of Cavendish.'

It seems that the citizens of Cavendish continued to pursue their policy of trying to deter criminal behaviour. In 1836 two men were sentenced to transportation for life for stealing two lambs. In the same year another man was given 7 years transportation for stealing four sacks of wheat from the granary of Joseph Stammers Garrett. In 1843 a man aged 62 was charged with stealing tools. The report states that in view of his age mercy was shown and he was sentenced to one month imprisonment. Six years later two younger men, aged 14 and 17, were charged with stealing a silver fork and were sentenced to six months imprisonment and a whipping.

By October 1860, there was a constable based in the village and the magistrates said they were determined to support him. They fined a labourer from Cavendish 15 shillings (75 pence) for being drunk and disorderly and sent a man from Glemsford to prison for 7 days for being drunk and riotous at Cavendish. It was, according to the bench, the custom of the young men of Glemsford to go to the parish of Cavendish and misbehave in a disorderly manner.

In the 1920's the policeman was based at No 5, The Terrace. His name was Mr Nice and his nickname was 'not very'. He was followed by Mr Cheeseman. One of his duties was to go to the farms at Colts Hall and Wales End to check the animal movement records. Another of his responsibilities was checking guns.

Later on a police house was built for the village and was located next to the Memorial Hall and is now known as The Crickets. Mr Copsey and later Mr Andrews were based there. The house was sold in 1979.

In 1987 a neighbourhood watch scheme was set up and organised by Ken Christian through liaison with the police. He recruited a team of local contacts to facilitate a network of communication through the village. Although Ken moved away the scheme still continues.

Cavendish also has a beat officer who provides a point of contact for general police matters and makes a regular and helpful contribution to the Parish Magazine. This is in addition to the emergency service available from Police HQ in Martlesham.

Electricity

The village received an electricity supply in October 1931 and the local newspaper reported 'quite a mild sensation' when it was first switched on at dusk. Adults and children alike had heard a rumour about the lighting up of the village and so at 6pm all were looking out for the event.

The late Don Angel recalled seeing his first electric light outside the George Inn. It appeared to him and his friend like a light in a glass bottle but try as they might they were unable to blow it out.

Prior to this date lighting was mainly in the form of oil lamps. Even longer ago lighting was by candles or tapers and some of the older properties in the village still show where the tapers singed the wood.

Fire Service

An early record shows that during the 18th century buckets of water were kept ready in the church tower for dowsing fires in the village. The first local appliance was acquired in Clare in 1844. In September of that year a fire occurred in a hayloft at Blacklands Farm. Everyone available went to help and managed to quench the flames so that by the time the fire engine from Clare arrived the fire was out.

A subscription fund was set up in 1846 by the residents of Foxearth, Cavendish and Pentlow to raise the funds to buy their own fire engine. The response was so positive that a powerful engine was bought and kept at Rectory House, Pentlow. The excellent engine and efficient fire brigade were praised after attending a fire in 1853 in nearby Pentlow.

Cavendish later obtained its own engine and attended a large fire at Houghton Hall in 1881 along with the Sudbury engine, when four stacks of wheat, straw and oats; two barns; stables; granary and equipment were destroyed.

The Cavendish engine was pulled by men and later by horses and at different times was kept at Barltrops the Blacksmiths (now the Sue Ryder shop), and at Blacklands Farm, and at Nether Hall.

Its rules and regulations include;

> 'Members of the Brigade shall only be allowed to ride on the engine to or from a fire.
>
> The Captain shall procure horses in case of need at a cost not exceeding 10/- each per day, provided they are efficient.

The restored fire engine which attended the blaze at Hyde Park Corner Cottages in 1971
Denise Davies

> The Brigade shall drill not less than once in three months, the drills being wet and dry alternately.'

The fire engine from Clare which was first on the scene at the huge blaze at the Hyde Park Corner Cottages on Easter Monday 1971 has recently been restored and in order to mark the anniversary was brought to the village over Easter weekend 2001.

Water

Before mains water, houses were dependent on water pumped manually from the nearest spring. In some cases this meant carrying water by bucket to fill the copper which was used to heat the water. Other properties were lucky since they had a spring near their back door and water could be pumped directly into a holding tank in the roof. Ruth Steed can remember that it took fifty strokes of the pump to raise sufficient water to fill the tank each evening. Ernie Playle can recall the location of many of the springs in the village.

Mains water supply was installed in the village during the 1950s and this provided a welcome respite from the drudgery of collecting water.

Mains drainage was also completed in the village during this period. When the workmen were digging up the road for the pipes on one occasion they inadvertently dug into natural springs so the trenches kept filling up with water. In order to keep them clear pumps were fitted all along the High Street and were on all day and evening. At night someone had to go round turning them off to ensure that people had chance to sleep.

Many youngsters used to swim in the millpond near Pentlow Mill seventy years ago. It was with some surprise that one of them learned recently that before mains drainage the untreated sewage from houses went straight into the Stour. Today regular testing of water quality takes place at Pentlow Bridge by staff from the National Rivers Authority.

The village pond was kept clean for the animals which grazed on the green to drink there. It was also used by cattle being driven to market. Later traction engines and threshing tackle stopped there to fill up their water tanks. Horse and carts could be driven through as there was a firm foundation at either side. This was the site of a tragedy when Richard Wells, aged 43, and his horse were electrocuted on 4th May 1938. A lorry laden with hay had collided with the overhead power line and the broken cable had fallen into the pond where Richard's horse was drinking. The horse had trodden on the wire and was electrocuted and Richard died trying to assist.

In recent years, the Waver, as the pond is known, has been used by ducks and moorhens. There are plans to undertake a major renovation programme.

Today the River Stour is part of a complex water control system run by the National Rivers Authority. The pumping station at Wixoe was opened by the Queen in 1971 and this secures the water supply to North London and the Colchester area via reservoirs around Colchester. In effect the Stour becomes a pipeline to the Abberton reservoir among others. At times of drought or flood the sluices at Wixoe help control the water flow. The higher temperature of the River Ouse water flowing into the lower reaches of the colder Stour at times causes algae to form which appears like froth.

TRANSPORT

Although Cavendish is situated on the north bank of the River Stour, the river has never been navigable here. Communication has been mainly by road and for a period by rail. In the 17th, 18th and early 19th centuries journeys took place by carrier or coach, often linking into a main stage coach route to larger towns. As Cavendish is on the A1092 this links it to the A1307 (formerly A604) in the west and A134 to the east.

A directory of **Stage Coach Services** in 1836 gives the following timetable for the Royal Mail Coach from Norwich to London Daily. A Cavendish person could join at Bury St Edmunds.

Norwich	depart	5.00pm
Attleborough	...	6.38pm
Thetford	...	8.13pm
Bury St Edmunds	...	9.33pm
Newmarket	...	11.21pm
Littlebury	...	1.31am
Bishops Stortford	...	2.59am
London GPO	arrives	6.29am

Records do not relate the descriptions by passengers of such a long journey on unsurfaced roads, nor do they detail the punctuality or otherwise of such a service.

In 1855 a William Byford was listed as being a carrier to London via Sudbury each day. Although William still lived in the village in 1885 he was no longer a carrier, that role having been superseded by the railway.

Two main rail routes had been built - Cambridge to London and Bury St Edmunds to London, and Cavendish was fortunate that a track was laid to link the two. Cavendish **railway** station opened on 9th August 1865. A map of 1783 indicates that this was the site of Cavendish Place, home of Shadrach Brise who died in 1699. His memorial is built into the wall of the north aisle of the church. The line was part of the Colchester, Stour Valley, Sudbury and Halstead Railway or C.S.V.S & H.R for short. In the 1890s it became part of the Great Eastern Railway and the letters on its rolling stock were changed to G.E.R. In 1923 this joined the London and North Eastern Railway - L.N.E.R - and eventually British Rail - B.R - until it closed on 4th March 1967 after 102 years of service. The freight service had ceased on 28th December 1964.

TRANSPORT

A Great Eastern timetable of 1895 shows:-

Cambridge	depart	10.40 am
Haverhill	...	11.20 am
Cavendish	...	11.44 am
Long Melford	...	11.59 am
Sudbury	...	12.05 pm
Marks Tey	arrive	12.37 pm
	depart	12.48 pm
Liverpool Street	arrive	2.10 pm

There were four other passenger trains each day plus goods trains. The journey to London could be made in the opposite direction to Cambridge and from there to London.

A timetable for the late 1950's also demonstrates this:-

Depart Cavendish – 6.47 am – change Marks Tey
- arrive Liverpool Street – 8.46 am

Depart Cavendish – 6.46 am – change Cambridge
- arrive Liverpool Street – 9.38 am

In the late 1950's there were thirteen passenger trains a day - Monday to Friday - calling at Cavendish including the two examples above. In addition freight trains used the station.

Depart Cavendish 6.47 am to Ipswich via Sudbury (onward connection to London)

Depart Cavendish	9.23 am	to Colchester	10.13 am
Depart Cavendish	11.50 am	to Sudbury	12.05 pm
Depart Cavendish	2.39 pm	to Sudbury	2.54 pm
Depart Cavendish	4.30 pm	to Sudbury	4.45 pm
Depart Cavendish	6.30 pm	to Colchester	7.31 pm
Depart Cavendish	8.48 pm	to Colchester	9.37 pm

Via Haverhill to Cambridge

Depart Cavendish   6.46 am to Cambridge (onward connection to London)

Depart Cavendish	9.47 am	to Cambridge	10.44 am
Depart Cavendish	12.45 pm	to Cambridge	1.42 pm

117

Depart Cavendish	3.45 pm	to Cambridge	4.43 pm
Depart Cavendish	5.15 pm	to Cambridge	6.16 pm
Depart Cavendish	6.48 pm	to Cambridge	7.43 pm

Stations on each route included
London, Colchester, Marks Tey, Chappel and Wakes Colne, Bures, Sudbury, Long Melford, Glemsford and Cavendish.

and

Cavendish, Clare, Stoke by Clare, Sturmer, Haverhill, Bartlow, Linton, Pampisford, Shelford, Cambridge and London.

Examples of fare and journey times are as follows:-

Sudbury to London	3rd Class return fare		Time
1849	6/9d	(34p)	148 mins
1856	8/-	(40p)	135 mins
1883	6/6	(32½p)	105 mins
1894	4/11½	(25p)	97 mins
1922	4/11½	(25p)	98 mins
1930	7/5d	(37p)	99 mins
1939	7/11d	(40p)	96 mins
1947	12/3d	(61p)	111 mins

2nd Class

1956	9/3d	(46p)	93 mins
1965	16/-	(80p)	83 mins
1969	15/6d	(77½p)	80 mins

Mr William Tharby worked at Cavendish Station for 48 years between 1905 and 1953. His wife worked as the station crossing keeper for 18 years. They lived at the Gate House until Mr Tharby's retirement in 1953 when he moved to Lower Street.

Whilst at the station, Mr Tharby had many interests in addition to his work. He used to graft apple trees and roses and grow flowers such as gladioli which he could then sell. He had between thirty and forty beehives and his honey was very popular especially during the war when sugar was in short supply.

Mr Tharby's son, Alfred, remembers that as a boy one of his jobs was to use the pump at the end of what is now Pentlow Drive, to fill up the water supply for the house and station yard. Water was also needed for the cattle which were carried on the goods trains. Alfred Tharby used to earn 3d (just over 1p) for helping to accompany the cattle safely to Pentlow. Other freight carried coal and sugar beet.

Cavendish Station

The station seems to have been a busy place with constant movement of goods. The railway enabled more visitors from further afield to come to the village and stay for short breaks. It also helped to reduce the comparative isolation of the village by giving the opportunity to visiting new places. The regular rail service was popular because it enabled young mothers to go shopping in Sudbury. Since prams were much more bulky than today's pushchairs, they were put in the guards van whilst the women travelled with their babies in the carriages.

Many people continued to use pony and traps and horse and carts for local journeys and deliveries but the competition from motor vehicles increased. Dr Ritchie had one of the first cars in the village and over the years drove many different makes including Albert, Angus Sanderson, Clyno, Standard, Citroen, Daracq and Alvis. Eventually in 1938 he acquired a Rover 12.

The **road** through the village was tarmaced around 1923. Mary Turkentine's brother, Herbert now 88, can remember the work being carried out. He was about 10 years old at the time. The chippings were brought to Cavendish by the railway and then taken to the new road by horse and two wheeled cart. The rest of the road making equipment was drawn by horse and cart, including that on which the tar was boiled. When all the work was complete, Herbert recalls having a good game of marbles on the new surface.

A 20 seater charabanc

During the 1920's, Cuttings of Glemsford installed a petrol pump near number 55 High Street, which reflected the growing demand. Evening bus parties to dances or to the cinema at Sudbury were catered for by Mr Bert Brown in his 20 seater charabanc. Longer journeys were provided for by Chinnery's or Long's coaches.

TRANSPORT

Bolden's garage

In the 1950's Mr Bolden had a garage selling petrol and repairing cars. It was an agency for Ford and Triumph cars. This was situated at the end of the High Street near the Green and where today is found Chinnerys and the antique shop.

Today there are two bus companies providing a service to the village. On every day except Sunday a Beeston's bus travels backwards and forwards from Haverhill to Sudbury starting about 7 am and finishing about 6 pm.

A Chambers bus journeys from Sudbury to Bury St Edmunds via Clare once a day leaving Bury at 1.30 pm. On Sundays and Bank Holiday Mondays a Chambers bus travels from Ipswich to Haverhill via Lavenham, Kersey, Long Melford and Clare providing the opportunity to visit friends or enjoy the ride.

Poole Street before road widening

Over the years traffic levels have increased and the A1092 has been widened to deal with the flow. In 1967 the road was widened in Poole Street near Green End and two cottages were pulled down.

In 1971 notices were served on the owners of all the properties between Peacocks and Melcott on the High Street and all the houses north of Lower Street up to the Memorial Hall relating to a road widening scheme.

All the properties lost substantial parts of their front gardens, some of which used to stretch to the white line in the middle of the present road. The line of the old road can still be seen as the parking area and roadway near the United Reformed Church.

TRANSPORT

Lower Street before road widening

TRADE AND INDUSTRY

Local merchants throughout England produced their own low value brass and copper coins for the use of local people. These coins were called **tokens** and were made between 1648 and 1672.

Several of these coins were made by innkeepers and there are three local examples - The Black Lion at Glemsford in 1669; the Half Moon at Clare (now a house) and the White Hart at Long Melford (now a Persian carpet shop). On the front of the token there is usually the name of the merchant with a sign of the nature of his business. An axe was the sign of a butcher and a leg with high boots the sign of a bootmaker. On the back was the date and place of origin.

Cavendish token

Cavendish token (reverse) - James Ellis 1669
Andrew Norman

There were seven tokens produced in Cavendish;

1. William ALCOCK – 1657. He was later a trustee of the free school established in 1696 by the Rector Thomas Grey for fifteen poor children.
2. Daniel CHICKELL – 1657. He owned lands at Pentlow.
3. James ELLIS – 1669. His token is illustrated. It shows a pair of scales, said to represent justice and honesty. He was also a school trustee.
4. James FITCH. Shows a pair of scales.
5. Thomas FULLER. A blazing star. He was a man of substance and left an extensive will.
6. John MERRILLS – 1664. Sign of a blazing sun.
7. John WOODS – 1663. An Oak tree with leaves and acorns and 1665 with three crowns on a Royal Oak. He was a Say maker i.e. a cloth like serge. In his will he left orchards and barns to his family.

TRADE AND INDUSTRY

Clare had seven tokens and of interest to Cavendish is the token of William Colte 1664. The Coltes had long connections with the village having given their name to Colts Hall formerly the manor of de Greys.

When Cavendish Maltings were being converted into dwellings a token was found. This was inscribed with the initials JSG, those of the owner of the Maltings, Joseph Stammers Garrett. It is likely these tokens were included in the weekly wage to be used for the purchase of a pint of beer.

Home deliveries have always played an important part in village life. Some early memories of Cavendish residents help to illustrate this. Milk was delivered by horse and cart by Mr Orbell and his dog. He had a large churn from which he scooped the milk using a large jug. Mrs Deal, on the other hand, used to pull her cart with a churn on it. Bread was delivered by Mr Pettitt with his horse and cart. Mr Tharby used to spend his school lunch hour delivering bread for Creane's the baker. He also collected the papers from the train at 7 am and would have delivered them as far as Poole Street by 8am in time for him to go to school.

Home deliveries for Cavendish

Today the service continues with deliveries from a mobile butcher, fishmonger and shop, coalman, milkman and postman. The mobile Library calls fortnightly. A fish and chip van visits on a Saturday evening. The village shops provide deliveries of papers, groceries, greengroceries and flowers.

Cavendish was once described as a very self sufficient village.

During the 19th and 20th centuries a huge range of occupations, trades, crafts and businesses were represented here. Many of the crafts and trades referred to such as straw plaiter, woolcomber, and knap weaver are unfamiliar to us today, whilst others such as cooper, collar and harness maker and wheelwright show how changes in transport have affected the demand for such skills.

Joe Hale was born in Cavendish in 1912. He described to his granddaughter, Sarah, in 1978 some of his **memories of old Cavendish** which are detailed below together with recollections of other residents.

> 'We are starting at the Clare end of Cavendish, walking down into the village, right down the street as far as the village goes, and then back up the other side. When I was a little boy the furthest house that did any business was the 'Fir Trees' later on that was turned into a barber's shop. I used to go there to have my hair cut.'

The Fir Trees public house

This led to the story that Cavendish had the best groomed men in the area! The landlord of the 'Fir Trees', Mr Barham, had been in the army and one young man, newly up from London was most disappointed to receive a short back and sides instead of the latest 'Tony Curtis' style he had anticipated.

> 'Walking into the village and turning down the lane we went over the railway crossing where the trains went over the road, and so on down to Cavendish village mill.'

The railway crossing was called after the people who occupied the crossing house, Copmans Lane, Haddocks Lane and Johnsons Lane. The old gate keeper before Mr Johnson took over used to forget to open the gates and the train would go straight through sending the gates flying. It is now called Mill Lane.

Cavendish Mill

> 'Back on the main road we pass several houses where 3 or 4 families lived, they've now been turned into one separate house. There's a big gap from what we used to call 'Workhouse Street', up into the main village – the first real village activity was the first cottage on the right where Mrs Maxim used to live, and there she had a laundry; she used to take in a lot of washing for women, for different houses, several women worked there. A little further on there was Mr Rice's shop, a painter. He used to mix his own paints, I've been there when he had a machine, and you put the stuff in and turned the handle, and the paint came out of the other end. From there we come to the house where I was born; the Butcher's shop with the slaughterhouse at the back.'

Cattle and sheep grazed on the village green before being taken across the road to Hale's the butchers. In 1969 flood water on Hale's corner was very deep and some piglets and chickens had to be rescued. Paddy Godfrey the policeman, Len Brown, Fred and Mary Turkentine, Joe Hale and others waded waist deep in water in order to rescue them.

Frank Hale and son – family butcher

Sheep grazing on the green

'Then to one side of us was a shoe repairer, and also opposite we had another shoe repairer.'

Mr Perkins in the first and Mr Thompson in the one opposite.

'About two doors along where it is now (1978) the 'Grapevine' used to be a private school, run by Miss Clarke. Next door was Mr Barltrop, he had a blacksmiths shop, they used to shoe the horses there and they also had a general shop where they sold spades, forks, mole traps, wire netting, lawn mowers etc. Two doors on was a Men's Institute, where as a young man I used to go. We played draughts, dominoes, billiards and read papers; there were weekly magazines there, and that was also where the village paper was sold. Next door was a little general stores where Mr Newman lived, that's where I got most of my sweets as a little boy. I used to go in when he was having his dinner, and the old man would be munching – and they used to put the sweets in paper bags in those days and he used to blow the bag open - and you had half his dinner in with his sweets, as all the crumbs blew off his mouth.'

G Barltrop – blacksmith advertisement

Cavendish Reading Room and Institute

After Newman's came Little's and later the 'Duck or Grouse', supplying groceries and newspapers to the village.

> 'Next door to him was the Grammar School, it wasn't open in my days, my uncle and father both went there. Two doors further on was another bakers, Mr Pettitt, he used to deliver his bread with a horse and cart, and he had a huge hood that went right over the top of his cart, like a pram has, and a lot of us boys, when he went by the Green, used to hang on the back of the cart, and we could stop the pony. The old man used to get his whip and try to hit us, but when he'd got his hood up he could not see us. Next door to him was a currier, a place where they supply leather; he used to supply leather to the local shoe repairers.'

Cavendish Cinema on the site of part of the old Grammar School

Bradley Parker later sold second hand furniture here, much of which was displayed on the pavement. He kept chickens and would pay children to glean corn from the fields for them. Elizabeth Tea Rooms were then a popular tourist attraction with many coaches stopping. This was followed by 'Alphonso's' an Italian Restaurant.

> 'Then the village pond. Then there was a big house known as the Old Rectory, now the Sue Ryder Home. Down the village further on the right where they've built the bungalows used to be a big stack of faggots. Mr Garrett used to buy these faggots off the farmers and they made huge stacks with them and took them across to the Maltings to make fuel for the fire. A little further down where Mr Underwood lived,

F W Brown, Baker and confectioner – now The Old Bakery

he used to make shoes. Next door to him was the wheelwright, they used to mend wheels for wagons and carts. Next door was a big row of houses built by Mr Garrett, and the first one was where the policeman lived. Further down was where Mr Ives lived, another painter. The next house now called 'Full of Beans', was another private school, Miss Garrett kept that, 10 or 15 children went there, they used to come from other villages in horses and traps every morning and someone would come for them in the afternoon, the lessons were in the morning. Further down the street was another shoemaker.'

A former Post Office standing next to Granby Cottage in the 19th century

There were many shoemakers in Cavendish. Frank Purdy along with his father had carried on the trade of clog and patten maker and also soled boots with wooden soles. They delivered their goods as far as Norwich by horse and cart. Frank carried on the business as a cab proprietor and gave this up when motor transport increased. He died in 1937 aged 85 years.

> 'Next door to him was a blacksmith, Mr Rushbrook, 'Old John' we used to call him, a big, strong man. Next door was another bake house where they made bread and also sold sweets. Twenty yards further on was the Chapel. In my young days that was very strong, very often it was difficult to get a seat. Next door was the Maltings, also belonging to Mr Garrett, but they weren't used much, they were eventually pulled down and two houses built there.'

The Maltings were sold in 1923 to Ernest Graham. He pulled them down and built two houses on the site, selling them in 1926. Further along Lower Street were three thatched cottages where Seymour House and Green Gables now stand. The cottages burnt down in 1970. During the 1930s a shoemaker had a small workshop in the centre cottage. He used to walk to work from his home in Glemsford. He was called 'Sleepy' Underwood because he talked and moved so slowly. He is fondly recalled by Mr Tharby. Before Mr Tharby's marriage over 60 years ago Sleepy told him he couldn't afford to buy them a present but his gift was the wish 'May God treat you as you treat each other'. It has never been forgotten.

> 'Further on the same side was a Thatcher. Then we come to the Railway Arms and the station.'

The Railway Arms was built in 1864 by Mr T Skelton on the corner of Lower Street and Pentlow Lane, near the site of the new railway station, which was opened in 1865. In 1879 it was run by George Smith and in the 1930's by Mrs Alice Brunning. Mr Alfred Tharby remembers that as a boy he used to catch eels using night lines and sell them to Mrs Brunning who put them on the menu for the day.

The railway closed down in 1967 but the Railway Arms continued for another thirty years and is now a private house.

> 'I've seen 100 people come off the trains there at holiday time, also the goods yard which was very busy, the bullocks we bought at Bury came by train and we had to drive them up the street, that was quite a game, also the sheep, they used to run up people's yards. The last house in the village towards Glemsford was the manse, the chapel parson lived there. Now we turn and come back on the other side of the road. The first

The Railway Arms showing the wood stored at the carpenter's and undertaker's yard opposite.

> building is the Memorial Hall. In those days it was half as big and was known as the chapel school, 20 or 30 children went there. Next door was the carpenter's shop and the undertaker, Mr Graham. Two or three men worked there.'

Later Bob Page carried on the business.

> 'On the corner of Water Lane lived my aunt, she used to sell a little meat which we sent down from the shop where I lived. Down Water Lane at Blacklands Farm where we had to go to see the doctor. Nobody had a car in those days and it was a long walk for people to go to see the doctor. You had to sit in a tiny waiting room, a little cold place, just a shelter over 2 walls. Back in the village, nearly opposite the old Blacksmiths was a yard. In my young days there was a factory there and they used to make matting, they were quite busy, 4 or 5 women worked there.'

The matting factory made coconut fibre mats for the Chrysler car company in America. It was in production between the wars. A horsehair factory was also based here. For a number of years from the mid 1880's a factory making silk on steam driven looms was in production here.

> 'A little further up was Mr Brewster's General Stores. He used to go round with a horse and cart until he got a van, he used to supply oil and candles etc.'

Later on it became 'Bean's', general store, groceries and drapery. 'Tricker's' electrical store was also there and had the first colour TV in the village.

> 'The next little shop up was where the Post Office used to be. Mr Evans kept the Post Office; he also delivered the letters himself. There were two other postmen in the village at the time. One of them walked down to Pentlow and all over – from Cavendish Mill up one hill and down the other to Pentlow Mill.'

Felix Angel began work as an ancillary postman in 1902 and covered the area as far as Wales End on foot. After completing 22 years of service he was given a bicycle and the Pentlow area was added to his route. He retired after $52^{1}/_{2}$ years service never having missed a delivery.

> 'Then Mr Tatum, he did the other delivery to the outlying farms, he walked miles, poor old boy, every morning. Some people had newspapers delivered, so he had to go round every morning with them. Nearly opposite to the policeman's house was a little shop where they used to sell sweets. Up a little higher was Mr Creane's bake house, they used to deliver bread in the village, they also had a busy little general shop, and they used to make a lot of cakes, iced ones at Christmas time.'

Around Christmas time on a Wednesday when there was only one baking, villagers took their big hams to be baked in the oven. Three generations of the Creane family ran the business.

> 'Next door was another wheelwright, old Smith's, he used to do blacksmiths work as well. Then a little up was Mr Brockwell's builder's yard. The building he used as a building shed had been previously used as a skittle yard, because his house had been built on the site of a pub – I think it was called 'The White Horse.'

The White Horse was situated in the High Street next door to The Bull and had a frontage of 103 feet. The building stretched from The Bull to the driveway of the present Post Office. The brew house, granary yard, gardens and outbuildings stood at the rear.

The White Horse Inn was owned by John Churchyard and bequeathed to his daughter in a will dated 1877. The Inn provided stabling and Peggy Jackson's father used to leave his pony and trap there when he played cricket. In 1908 the licence of the Inn was refused (reason unknown) and compensation awarded by the Suffolk Licensing Committee. The following year Mrs Ann Coe (daughter of John Churchyard) sold part of the premises, on the site of which now stand Southleigh and Norfolk House, to Mr O Thompson. The remaining 59 foot

The Bull and The White Horse

frontage was sold to Mr Thomas Brockwell a builder who erected a house, 'Brockholm', in 1922. This was subsequently renamed Stormont in 1964.

> 'Next door to him was Mr Thompson, the harness maker he was also an insurance agent, a man worked for him.'

Oliver Thompson retired from the business at the beginning of the Second World War. He was the third generation of his family to be saddler and harness maker. His father died when the eldest of his four sons was 17. Their grandfather supervised and the four boys ran the business. It prospered and the brothers joined businesses in Shrewsbury, Long Melford and Oxford leaving Oliver working in Cavendish.

> 'and next door to that was 'The Bull' another busy pub where they used to brew their own beer.'

This is sited in the High Street and provides a popular venue for locals and visitors alike. It used to brew its own beer in a brew house at the back until the 1920's.

There is a list of previous landlords on the wall near the fire.

In September 1929 there was a well publicised incident at the Bull when Nora Plumb, aged 25, who had worked there as a bar maid and domestic help since leaving school, was shot by her admirer George Newton Morley, who then shot himself. Morley was buried in Cavendish cemetery and Nora at Pentlow churchyard.

'Up a little higher we come to the present newsagents, that was a watchmaker's shop, Mr Carter's. We used to worry the poor old man. He used to sit with a little thing in his eye so he could peer into those watches, we used to stand outside and keep tapping the rail round his window, he used to get really cross. Opposite the pond we come to Mr Clark, the big grocer's shop. Nearly next door was the Maltings which was always busy with 5 or 6 men working from 7am to 7pm. We used to take our bacon and hams over to hang in the Maltings to get dry.'

Sam and Henrietta Garrett had taken over the malting and milling business from their father Joseph in 1898 whilst he continued farming. The two large maltings' chimneys could be seen from Pentlow Hill. Percy Bullock cleaned the chimneys out every week with his brothers Stan and Bert. After Sam retired, Haslers, the corn and seed merchants used the Maltings for dressing grass seeds and pulses. In September 1971 a factory for RMS Audio opened up. It produced radio parts and offered employment mainly for assemblers and solderers.

In 1979 permission was granted for the Maltings to be converted into dwellings.

The Maltings after its conversion into dwellings

'Further on was the 'George', the hotel run by Mr Deeths who also used to brew his own beer.'

It used to be a popular venue due to its position near the green but after a recent change of ownership its future is currently uncertain.

Lot 2.

THE

Fully Licensed Freehold Property,

KNOWN AS

THE GEORGE HOTEL

A well-known Commercial and Posting Establishment, pleasantly situate on the main road, with Southern aspect, overlooking the Green, in the Village of Cavendish, and within half-a-mile of Cavendish Station (G.E.R.), comprising a

BRICK, PLASTER AND TILED
COMFORTABLE HOUSE,

CONTAINING

ON GROUND FLOOR.—Large Parlour, Smoke Room, Bar, Tap Room, Kitchen, Scullery and Two Cellars.

ON FIRST FLOOR.—Sitting Room, Commercial Room, Six Bedrooms and Closet.

The Outbuildings
include a
BRICK and TILED BREWERY

(equipped with 6½ Coombs Brewing Plant); Brick and Tiled Spirit Cellar; Cart Shed with Granary over; Two-stall Stable with Two Loose Boxes and Hay Loft over; Slated lean-to Coach House; Brick and Tiled Nag Stable; lock-up Coal House; open Shed and a Slated Pigsty.

A Well with Pump provides an excellent supply of water.

This Property is now let to Mr. Frederick Deaves, who is under notice to quit for the purpose of this Sale.

Certain Tenant's Fixtures, including the Beer Engines and Fittings, Kitchen Range and Heating Stove in Scullery, are claimed by the Tenant. These the Purchaser will have to take over by Valuation in the usual way and in addition be required to pay the sum of £30 for the Brewing Plant.

Included in this Lot is the adjoining

BRICK, PLASTER & TILED COTTAGE,

Let to Mr. Robert Everett, who is under notice to quit for the purposes of Sale.

Sale particulars 1920 – The George Hotel

Mr Chinnery standing outside his butcher's shop – now an antique shop

> 'Next door to this was what used to be the garage, but in my young days was a butchers shop, with a slaughter house. Then we come up the road to the Rectory. That was where Canon Barnard lived, he was the Reverend Barnard in my young days. He was the parson for a long while. On the green was 'The Five Bells'. It used to be a little thatched pub in those days. It was pulled down and a new house built, but they still thatched it'.

In 1739 the Five Bells was left to Mary Briant under the will of Robert Harnass who was then living at Green End.

The Five Bells stands at the top of the green near the church from whose belfry it originally acquired its name.

> 'On the top of the green was the Church School. When I went there, there were about 110 children. There were also 30 going to the Chapel School down the street'.

If Joe Hale had continued past the church and turned into Colts Hall Lane, just past Nether Hall on the left he would have been surprised to have found a vineyard. Basil Ambrose had researched the feasibility of growing vines in the area and his plans had come to fruition. He had hired a car and set off on his

The Five Bells

researches, travelling north from the southern Rhine in Germany. He discovered that the river Thames is on a similar latitude to the Moselle and that black grapes need more sun.

On reaching Colmar on the Rhine he made contact with one of the biggest growers and also sellers of wine. He decided to grow the Mueller Thurgau grape because its qualities would suit the environment of the Stour Valley. He bought the vines in January 1972 and returned in April to collect them.

There were sufficient vines to plant up 10 acres of land and with help from his farming colleagues they achieved this in a week. This acreage doubled the size of the vineyards in England at the time.

The first crop in 1974 was a light one but produced a dry white wine. It was a very good year in 1975 and proved to be the best yielding and top prize winning wine. The yield of 1976 was the biggest with 33 tons of grapes being picked. Many well known people have enjoyed Cavendish Manor Wine. The Queen Mother was presented with a case when she came to open the Sue Ryder Museum in 1979 and customers included Hammond Innes, Leonard Rossiter, Paul Eddingten and Enoch Powell. Production ceased in 1990.

ORGANISATIONS AND ACTIVITIES

Many activities are undertaken in the village today reflecting a wide range of common interests. Although the type of activity may have altered, the fact that people have always busied themselves and taken part is evident in documents relating to the past as well.

It is not possible to detail all the organisations and activities past and present but it is hoped the following will provide a flavour of what made Cavendish the place it was and what makes it the place it is today.

Organisations which no longer exist in Cavendish were many and varied and suited an array of eclectic tastes.

Cavendish Literary & Debating Society was formed in January 1933 and the minute books make interesting reading. Six officers were appointed including president, chairman, secretary and treasurer. A list of fourteen rules was also drawn up and accepted. These related to membership, subjects for debate and the procedure for each discussion. Members could invite two guests who could speak but were not allowed to vote. When the chairman stood, a speaker had to cease addressing the meeting and be seated. The society began by meeting fortnightly with over thirty people in attendance. The first topic for debate was the proposal 'that in the opinion of this house married women should not hold salaried posts'. Some of those present did not vote, but the motion was passed with a majority of eleven.

Other subjects covered in debates included:-

> 'that economy cuts as passed by the present government are unsound'.
> (for 20, against 9).
> 'that professionalism in sport should be abolished'.
> (for 14, against 12).
> 'that buses are preferable to rail transport'.
> (for 7, against 16).

After a summer break meetings continued on a monthly basis, however as a result of the difficulty in finding speakers and falling attendances the Society closed in January 1934.

Later that year **Cavendish Dramatic Society** was formed and their first production was Bernard Shaw's 'The Devil's Disciple'. It was thought by some to have been a rather ambitious choice, but the critics were proved wrong and the performance was considered to be a great success.

The cast was as follows:-

Mrs Dudgeon	Phyllis Tillbrook
Essie	Jessie Andrews
Christopher Dudgeon	Andrew Ives
Minister Anderson	Victor Ives
Mrs Anderson	Kathleen Barltrop
Uncle Titus	Alfred Tharby
His wife	Katie Garrett
Uncle William	Ernest Johnson
His wife	Norah Brown
Lawyer Hawkins	Charles Creane
Richard Dudgeon	Joseph Hale
Sergeant	Alfred Tharby
Major Swindon	Robert Brown
General Burgoyne	Arthur Deeks
Chaplain	Dennis Barnard

The Rev J D Barnard was the producer and members of the cast and other local people helped with the costumes and stage arrangement.

The Society went on to take the play to Preston St Mary and Ipswich. Dr Ritchie offered to take some of the cast in his Riley. However, due to the Doctor's style of driving, one of them refused to return with him.

The Society reformed after the war and became known as **The Cavendish Players**. The group performed plays and comedies including 'Rookery Nook', 'Arsenic and Old Lace', 'She Stoops to Conquer', 'The Ghost Train' and 'Tons of Money'. It also presented a pantomime, 'The Glass Slipper'. The players received complimentary reviews with praise for the producer - Donald Bain, stage management - Charles Johnson and Geoffrey Jackson and performances by amongst others Arthur Deeks, Joe Hale, Angela Hillier and Alba Cutmore.

Later on productions were presented twice a year on Thursday, Friday and Saturday nights in the Memorial Hall. These proved very popular with audiences of up to 120 a night. On some occasions, after playing at Cavendish the productions moved on to the Theatre Royal, Bury St Edmunds, such as 'The Boyfriend' 1970, and 'The Prime of Miss Jean Brodie' 1971. A musical was written especially for the players in 1971 by Gerry Hicks entitled 'A Ring around Rosie', and was very well received.

After several of the production team and cast moved from the area or changed jobs and found they had less time to offer, the enthusiasm and commitment declined and the Players ceased in the mid 1980s.

Cavendish Players – December 1953 'Ambrose Applejohn's Adventure'

In a newspaper of 27th July 1908 there is a brief report of **Cavendish Flower Show** when the best allotment was won by Walter Mortlock. The best dish of boiled potatoes by a working man's wife was won by Mrs George Ives.

The second Cavendish Flower Show took place on the Rectory meadow (now Overhall), and was reported on 22nd July 1909. There were 25 entries for the allotments and classes for the following:-

> Potatoes, cabbages, lettuces, turnips, red carrots long, red carrots short, pod peas, spring onions, autumn onions, cucumber, rhubarb and a collection of vegetables.

The tug of war was won by a team from Houghton Hall.

One of the village traditions was for the **Annual Fair** held on the Green. Originally a cattle fair was held on the 11th June with the following two days for pleasure. Stalls were set up and entertainments were on offer. The cattle fair had become obsolete by the 1890s but the fair on the green continued through the first half of the 20th century.

RULES & REGULATIONS

FOR THE

PRESERVATION

OF THE

CAVENDISH VILLAGE GREEN,

By order of the Parish Council, under the Local Government Act, 1894.

1. That travellers be prohibited the use of the Green except at Annual Fair held on June 11th, when Amusement Proprietors may draw on for a period commencing at 12 o'clock noon on the 10th, and ending at 12 o'clock noon on the 15th of June in each year.

2. For the use of the Ground at Annual Fair, a charge of threepence per foot frontage of all Stalls, Swings, Roundabouts, etc., etc., and an additional charge of one Shilling on all Living Waggons, shall be levied on Owners, or person in charge of the same.

3. The Clerk to the Parish Council shall collect all moneys, give a receipt for same, and render account to the Parish Council.

Dated this 5th day of May, 1936.

MARTEN, SUDBURY

Rules and Regulations – Annual Fair

Before the **South Suffolk Show** had a more permanent venue it was held three times in Cavendish. As the Wickhambrook and South Suffolk Agricultural Association, their Annual Show was held at Blacklands Hall Meadow on 26th June 1937. The South Suffolk Show was again held at Blacklands Park on 8th May 1954 and on the third occasion at Scotts farm on 8th May 1965. Red and white Friesians 'caused a sensation' by winning four of the cattle championships.

In response to local interest three Cavendish **Gymkhanas** were held in the late 1970s in the grounds of Pentlow Hall Farm with entries from Cavendish and the surrounding area.

One of the more unusual village organisations was the **Cavendish and District Rabbit Clearance Society**. At a meeting in March 1960 it was reported that a full time warrener had exterminated more than a thousand rabbits between June and December the previous year. Records do not give any further information as to the duration of this particular society.

Village organisations have always tried to cater for all age groups.

Cavendish Pre-School Playgroup takes place three mornings a week, Wednesday to Friday, in the Jubilee Room of the Memorial Hall. It caters for children aged between 3 and 5 from Cavendish and neighbouring villages. It was started in the late 1960s with the aim of providing somewhere for 3 and 4 year olds from the village to make friends and play together before starting school, and one of its proudest possessions in those early days was a sandpit! Now the playgroup has its own purpose-built, safe, fenced-in, outdoor play area behind the Jubilee Room.

There are 5 members of staff and the playgroup is run by a committee of parents. A small amount is charged for each session and a number of fund-raising activities take place throughout the year. There is a mix of organised activities and free play, including craft work, art, pencil, number and letter skills, home corner, dressing-up, dough, sand water and physical play equipment, and jigsaws, puzzles and many toys. There is a book corner and musical instruments, and the children join in with and respond to stories, songs, rhymes and music. There is a playgroup outing in the summer and a party at Christmas.

From its modest beginnings as a social opportunity for pre-school children, the playgroup is now registered with Suffolk County Council, inspected by Social Services and OFSTED, and since September 1997 has been successfully working in partnership with Cavendish Primary School to provide school mornings for 4 year olds whereby two of their state-funded sessions are spent at the playgroup and the other three at school. There is now a 'parents and tots'

ORGANISATIONS AND ACTIVITIES

group for the under 3s which meets on a Monday morning, and a pre-school music and movement class takes place on Thursday afternoons. Playgroup itself has recently included one lunchtime session a week where children bring a packed lunch and stay and eat with the other children.

What was started by a couple of mothers over 40 years ago is now a busy and thriving playgroup providing a secure and stimulating environment in which pre-school children can develop and learn through play.

Once youngsters start school they became very involved in schoolwork and other school based activities. For young girls there is a **Brownie** pack which meets at the school. This was originally started by Miss Perry who in 1972 celebrated 50 years of service to the Guiding movement. It was she who started a **Guide** Company in Cavendish and organised camps. This was disbanded in the early 1960s and restarted in 1972 by Mrs Dunn. It continued for some time before ceasing and the members joined the very active company in Clare.

In 1971 Olive Bettinson started a **Cub** pack in Cavendish. This was very popular and continued until her retirement in 1985 when members moved to Clare. There has never been a **scout troop** in Cavendish. A troop was formed by Harold Ince in Clare in 1931 and young men who wish to join have always travelled there.

At present there is no **Youth Club** in the village. Over the years when the demand has existed and when the enthusiasm and commitment has been present among volunteers to organise one and among young people to attend, then a successful club has been achieved. Gladys Bettinson set up a Youth Club a long time ago and in 1985 Terry Forrester restarted it. It proved to be extremely popular with a membership of well over 60 with ages ranging from 9 to 15. They undertook a range of activities including paddling 3 lilos and 4 canoes on the River Stour from Sudbury to Bures, did a charity walk in Thetford Chase, and went camping. Through their enthusiasm they raised sufficient funds to purchase their own minibus. In more recent years Richard Burkitt helped to run another active group, staging pantomimes and other activities.

Groups for women include an active Women's Institute and the Cavendish Ladies. In the past a **Women's Bright Hour** met regularly at the United Reformed Church for many years and the **Mother's Union** had a group a long time ago.

The **Women's Institute** is a national movement linked with the Associated Country Women of the World, whose objectives are to improve and develop conditions of rural life by fostering social and educational activities.

James Jones

Women's Institute 2000

ORGANISATIONS AND ACTIVITIES

The Cavendish WI was formed in October 1926. Meetings are held each month and comprise either evening or afternoon activities or outings to places of interest. At the meetings in the Memorial Hall there are speakers or demonstrations on a range of subjects. Various activities are also held at County level and members can avail themselves of courses organised at the WI's own Denman College in Oxfordshire.

This year, 2001, the Cavendish Women's' Institute celebrated its 75th birthday. An Anniversary Dinner was held to which a founder member, past presidents and county officials were invited.

The Cavendish WI looks forward to the future with confidence. The WI provides friendship, encourages skills and gives members an insight into national and international issues through the resolutions passed at the National Annual Meeting.

The **Cavendish Ladies** originally developed in the early 1970's after the village grew with the building of new estates. The young mothers did not have a meeting place and it was decided to form an informal group to meet once a month to attend talks or to learn craft skills. The group met in the Garden Room at the George, paid a small membership fee and called themselves the 'Cavendishes'. Today the membership stands at forty-five. The group meets ten months a year on the third Monday. The annual fee covers the cost of the hire of the Memorial Hall and speakers and any money left at the end of the year is given, as before, to mutually agreed charities.

The pattern of activities usually comprises two coach outings, six lectures, often illustrated, a Christmas Lunch taken locally, and a joint meeting at Christmas with the WI for carols and readings. A flower arrangement is always prepared for St Mary's Church at Harvest Festival.

The group is now called The Cavendish Ladies and remains a very informal and fun loving meeting.

The Cavendish branch of the **Royal British Legion** was formed on June 6th 1947. Membership over the years has fluctuated; at one time it was more than 100 but is now down to 52.

The Legion fulfils a welfare role for any ex-serviceman, not only legion members. The branch has won cups and area certificates for work they have undertaken.

Life memberships, for services to the Royal British Legion, have been awarded to Charles Finch and Henry Fitch. Henry and his wife Doris carried the standard for over 45 years. They represented the branch at many functions and events including those at Windsor Castle, and at Hyde Park where they saw King George VI and his wife Queen Elizabeth.

In Cavendish the annual Remembrance Day Parade takes place on the nearest Sunday to 11th November at 2.45pm at The War Memorial on the green.

Meetings are held every 2 months on the 3rd Monday in the month in the Bull at 8pm.

The **Women's Voluntary Service** organisation developed at national level when in the late 1930's Lady Reading was called in by the then Home Secretary, Sir Samuel Hoare. He felt that in spite of the number of women's organisations none was exactly fitted for assisting with civil defence. Lady Reading's principle was that people should give their muscle, their sweat and their thought, rather than give their purse. By the end of 1938 the volunteers numbered over 32,000. Members throughout the country had a role to play in the war effort.

In Cavendish Mrs Ince organised the local WVS which helped to provide support in many aspects of local daily life. There were also first-aid and nursing classes. Peggy Jackson can recall making jam in the old brew house behind the Bull Inn. The WVS sent sugar to Mrs Ince, oil stoves were used and about 50 lbs of plum and raspberry jam was made. It then went to the NAAFI.

After the war the work of the WVS continued. Lady Reading heard of a member who had cooked 5 meals in her kitchen, put them in a pram and delivered them to neighbouring elderly people. Thus, from this small beginning the Meals on Wheels service began.

The WVS became the Women's Royal Voluntary Service in 1966. Mrs Rabett began the Meals on Wheels service in Cavendish in 1973. The WRVS provides a Meals on Wheels service on Tuesdays and Thursdays. It was organised by the late Margaret Wade but is now co-ordinated by Valerie Orr. Meals are provided by Clare Middle School and are delivered by volunteer drivers. If meals are required on other days of the week these are provided through other organisations.

A detachment of the **Red Cross** was started in 1944 by Gladys Bettinson and in 1947 a link of the Junior Red Cross was begun when 29 members enrolled.

The younger members were involved in learning basic first aid, visiting the old and sick, changing library books for the elderly and collecting items to be sent abroad.

The Cadet and Associate Members helped to train the juniors, attended First Aid and Home Nursing lectures, undertook community and hospital escort work and also organised a medical loan depot.

The latter service was provided well into the 1960's.

The elements of caring and service in the community present in the previously described organisations have continued in **Cavendish Care**. This was set up in 1987 and offers practical support, care, companionship and social activities to the elderly, ill or housebound, also a voluntary car service.

The over 60s **'Forget me Not' Club** which ran for a period from 1963 offered mainly social activities. This was organised by Miss Perry and Miss Shrive.

Between 1919 and 1935, the Cavendish and Pentlow Horticultural Society held regular meetings. The present **Cavendish and District Horticultural Society** was formed in 1961 by W W Jackson and Tom Ambrose. The shows were always held in late September about 2 weeks before the inter-village show. It was customary to invite those who had done well in the village show to submit entries on behalf of Cavendish. The inter-village show drew entries from villages as far afield as Kesgrave, Melton, Martlesham, Nedging with Naughton and Bacton. Competition was fierce and it was not unknown for entries to the inter-village show to be sabotaged by rivals. A small sprig of parsley moved out of place could be enough to lose first prize.

1961 First Annual Flower & Produce Show after the Horticultural Society re-formed

During the 1960's there were between 12 and 18 people on the committee of the Horticultural Society. Mr Fred Turkentine, the present Show secretary, is the only member of that original committee still serving. The annual dinners were quite grand affairs, held in the Memorial Hall and for which professional caterers were employed.

The present society has about 65 members and meetings are held monthly in the Memorial Hall. The annual programme includes guest speakers and garden visits. The Flower and Produce Show is held annually in September, with 131 classes in sections for vegetables, fruit, flowers, flower arrangement, home made wines, cookery, art and craft and a class for children under 14 years of age. Members and non-members compete in their classes for a total of 10 awards plus rosettes. The judges are from the Royal Horticultural Society. The Basil Ambrose Cup and Prize is awarded for the best front of house display (either garden or containers). This competition is open to all residents and is judged in July.

Over the years the **allotments** have been based at different sites in the village. A map of 1904 shows the allotments in Chimney Field behind Overhall. They were then on Peter's Field where Grey's Close is now situated. Ernie Playle can remember some smallholdings on Church Field on the way to Colts Hall. Alf Debenham kept pigs here to supply his butchers' shop. Ernie recalls some allotments behind Layfield on 'Workhouse Street'.

Mr & Mrs Evans, who ran the Post Office, now The Old Post Office, owned the allotments behind their home in the High Street. Mr Evans used to tell the gardeners to stop working if he found them there on a Sunday.

Len Johnson working on his allotment
Denise Davies

ORGANISATIONS AND ACTIVITIES

In order to ensure a permanent base for the allotments the Parish Council and Community Council bought the land from Mrs Evans and the Parish continues to administer them. There are twenty four allotments, most of which are in use. An annual rent is payable and allotment holders grow a wide variety of fruit and vegetables. Len Johnson who has been an allotment holder for more than forty years, together with some of the more experienced allotment holders are always happy to share their knowledge with newcomers.

The **St Mary's Church Flower Guild**, originally called the Church Decorators, was formed in January 1960 as a result of a meeting at Blacklands Hall, chaired by Mrs Helen Pawsey.

In order to raise funds to puchase flower arranging equipment, a combined Bridge and Whist Drive was held at Blacklands Hall. The sum of £53 18s 4d was raised.

In 1965 it was suggested that a water tap be connected into the church, however this has never materialised. In 1986 the Flower Guild organised a Coffee Morning and raised £127.38p. This sum was handed to the Parish Council (who are responsible for the closed churchyard) to help towards the cost of installing a water tap in the churchyard.

Throughout the years the Guild has been responsible for arranging flowers in the church, with special efforts made for Church Holy Days.

The Guild has also organised flower festivals and helped the fuchsia displays staged by the West Suffolk Fuchsia Fellowship in 1990, 1996 and 2001.

Cavendish Footpaths Association was launched at a meeting in the Memorial Hall in November 1993. It aims to improve footpaths locally, to encourage people to walk and familiarise themselves with these footpaths and to co-operate with farmers. The group meets for a walk on the afternoon of the first Sunday of every month. The Association has a representative on the Parish Council and it also liaises with the Rights of Way Officer based in Bury St Edmunds.

Cavendish Community Council was formed in 1967 to preserve, foster and improve the lifestyle of the community. By arranging social and fund raising events it becomes possible to give financial help to village organisations and projects. Events organised by the Community Council have included barn dances, fireworks on bonfire night, barbecues, cheese and wine evenings, arts and craft exhibitions, open gardens and quiz nights. Some projects which have benefited from the Community Council have been the swimming pool at the school, the Jubilee extension to the Memorial Hall, the village sign, the parish notice board, seats and litter bins, and grants to many of the village leisure and sporting organisations. After a break of some years the Community Council was reformed in the spring of 2000 with regular events such as a Gala weekend over August Bank Holiday, bonfire and firework display as well as senior citizens and children's Christmas parties.

In February 2001 a **Cavendish Local History Society** was formed with the intention of increasing knowledge and understanding of local history relating to Cavendish and the surrounding area through speakers and other activities.

In 1995 **Cavendish Cricket Club** celebrated its 60th anniversary at its current ground. The club had been in existence, however, for at least 70 years before it first played on Blacklands Hall Park Field.

The first record of cricket at Cavendish dates from 1867 in an edition of the Suffolk and Essex Free Press dated 25th July. Here a report and scorecard described a match between Cavendish and Sudbury. Sudbury could only make 26 runs and Cavendish totalled 331, batting on after they had won the match as was the practice in local cricket until as recently as the 1950's. The Free Press reports that Sudbury 'excused themselves by saying their best players could not come'. Rather than the familiar cricket tea, the players and their companions 'partook of an excellent luncheon at the George Inn'. Later that season the Free Press reported another win for Cavendish, this time against Stoke by Nayland. Both matches were played on a Tuesday, at the Cavendish ground, but it is not known where this was in the village.

Its seems likely that the club had been active much earlier on in the nineteenth century. It was certainly well enough established by 1867 to attract cricketers of some calibre. C G Wynch, scorer of 127 against Sudbury, played for Sussex, Essex and MCC during the 1850's and 1860's.

The club has since had an uninterrupted history except for the two World Wars. The major figure in the club's history is Tom Ambrose. He first played for Cavendish as a 14 year old in 1905 and was renowned as an aggressive batsman and fast bowler. He was selected to play for Suffolk in 1914 but the match was never played due to the outbreak of war. Between the wars there was no official Suffolk minor county side, but he was a leading figure in the unofficial Suffolk team, the Travellers. Tom Ambrose's feats of big hitting were legendary; he once smashed the roof slates near Framlingham College clock with what is considered to be the longest six ever hit at that ground.

Sam Garrett (1867 – 1955) was captain of the club for many years. He had one leg shorter than the other, and had to have a runner when at the wicket.

The Football Star of 3rd September 1913 records another match:-.

'Last Saturday a team of G.E.R. employees journeyed to Cavendish (a sleepy old village in the heart of Suffolk) to play the local team at cricket. It was a great day in the annals of the hamlet and practically the whole village turned out to see the merry group off at the station in the evening, the half hour wait was enlivened by the Londoners giving some realistic cake walk and rag-time exhibitions. "What ever be they doing", queried an ancient native as he surveyed the whirling arms and legs.'

In 1935 the Cricket Club moved to its current ground, having previously played at a number of fields including one near Nether Hall. Tom Ambrose had also played for Sudbury, Haverhill and Halstead during the 1920's and 1930's and the landowner only offered the lease to the new ground when Ambrose agreed to return to Cavendish to run the team. A thatched pavilion was built, the thatch being replaced by more easily maintained tiles in the 1960's. The new ground saw the start of a consistent improvement in playing standards and quality of opposition which was interrupted by the Second World War. The club ceased to function between 9th May 1940 and 24th May 1946 and the ground and pavilion suffered from neglect as a consequence. In the immediate post war years hard work and financial outlay restored and improved matters.

Cavendish cricket team captained by Tom Ambrose

Tom Ambrose continued as captain until 1957 and played his final match in 1961 at the age of 70. At the age of 60 he had scored an unbeaten 82 against Tendring Park. He continued to be involved with the club, both as president and umpire until his death in 1977.

The team's performance during this period was dominated by a number of players Tom Ambrose had introduced to the club. Maurice Finbow was a competitive wicketkeeper and consistently high-scoring opening bat from 1935 to the 1960's. Vic Keyton was an all-rounder and the club's groundsman. Ernie Playle was a medium-pace bowler of meteoric accuracy who took a club record 100 wickets in the 1962 series, but who perhaps is better known for taking 10 wickets for 27 runs at Sudbury in 1965.

The 1950's also saw the advent of Sunday cricket and a second eleven. During the 1960's Cavendish developed into one of Suffolk's strongest village teams, aided by a new practice wicket and better pitches. By 1970, league cricket had begun to percolate down to the village cricket scene, and in 1974 the club joined the Suffolk league, immediately winning Division II. Around this time the Cricket Week was introduced as were the mid-week knock-out competitions, and Mark Tate set the club batting records for an innings (178 in 1977), and runs in a season (1328 in 1979).

The club's fortunes have since see-sawed as the decline in local school cricket and financial pressures have stretched resources both on and off the field. Co-operation with Cavendish Football Club and hard work by, among others, Dave Siegert and Maurice Finbow resulted in further improvements to the pavilion and playing surfaces. The club benefited from a new bar, changing rooms, artificial wicket and net facilities. Fortunes also improved on the playing side as Cavendish won Divisions IV, III, II of the Essex-centred Lancaster Garage League in successive seasons between 1987 and 1989.

In the late 1990s the club were finding it hard to find players from within the village to fulfil their fixture commitments. They came to a mutually beneficial arrangement with Sudbury Wanderers who had the players but anxieties about the long term availability of their pitch. The two teams amalgamated and became Cavendish Wanderers in 1997 since when they have gone from strength to strength.

They joined the Hargreaves Two Counties Cricket Championship League, playing teams in Essex and Suffolk, in Division 7 and have already worked their way through to Division 5 which they join next season.

The club has grown with many new recruits and the Wanderers now field a 1st and 2nd XI. Regular fundraising events are held to maintain the facilities and to cover costs. Playing links have been established with Holland and Australia.

A previous secretary of the club, Clive Stewart received a letter in November 1983 from a Skeet McKay of Cavendish, Australia. This correspondence has continued for nearly 20 years and culminated in a visit by Cavendish, Australia to Cavendish, Suffolk to play cricket at the opening of the refurbished cricket pavilion in 1988 by the Duke of Devonshire. The match was declared a draw after rain stopped play.

In addition, an Australian touring team, Shepparton Cricket Club, played at Cavendish, Suffolk in June 1986. The tour was organised by Graham Gemmill and in the year 2000 another tour by Shepparton (now renamed the Wattlesprigs after an Australian native tree) visited Cavendish led by Steve and David Gemmill, sons of the late Graham.

Association football has a long history in Cavendish. It is known from some old newspaper cuttings that a football club existed as long ago as the 1890s and apart from two world wars has probably been in continuous existence ever since.

The records are clearer after the second war. In 1946 the **Cavendish Football Club** was re-established, with Messrs Dudley Payne of Blacklands Farm and Tom Ambrose as President and Vice-President respectively. The home ground was The Park as it was known then which is also the present sports ground. The team entered in the Sudbury and District League and also played in the Suffolk Junior and Lavenham Junior Cups. At that time players paid one shilling and non players five shillings per year to be members. Both players and supporters paid two shillings coach fare for away games, often well supported. Sometimes away games would generate several coach loads.

Funds were supplemented by various functions including an annual dinner when the meat would be supplied by slaughtering a pig or pigs raised by the club.

The club prospered having at one time two senior teams and a youth team. The catchment area for the club was generally Cavendish and Glemsford.

The facility was shared by the Cricket and Football Clubs on an informal basis for many years, not always amicably, it should be noted. The seasons overlap, and with football being played on the cricket outfield the results were not always pleasing to the cricketers. It is not possible to write about the football club without mentioning the Sports Club. In the mid 1980s the need became apparent to upgrade the facilities, but this could not be done without security of tenure. The ground is part of Blacklands Farm, at that time leased on a peppercorn rent. A new forty year lease was negotiated at a rent nearer to market value and index linked. This lease was signed by members of a board of trustees established for the purpose. These trustees in turn delegated the day to day operation of the club to a Sports Club Committee consisting of equal numbers of representatives from both the Cricket and Football Clubs. At the same time the area of the land leased was increased to allow for an additional football pitch and two more wickets for cricket. With the new lease responsibility for the maintenance of all aspects of the facility were clearly assigned to the Sports Club.

The Sports Club pays the rent, insurance and all common expenses, but until the year 2000 when a 200 raffle club was started had no independent income, all monies coming from the cricket and football clubs, who also pay their individual costs such as kit, referees etc.

With the secured tenure, Maurice Finbow provided funds to add dressing rooms, showers and toilets to the pavilion. The improved facility was opened by the Duke of Devonshire in May 1988.

Later a grant was obtained from the Football Association for the new football pitch which was graded and seeded but unfortunately due to the enormous amount of earth moving required to correct the gradient, the final flat area was some yards too short to meet the standards set by the Border League in which the team plays. Due to the help of a certain senior executive of a large civil engineering company the project came in below budget and left sufficient funds for the materials for a new kitchen and bar to be added to the pavilion entirely with volunteer labour. Later a referee's dressing room was fitted out in the Memorial Hall with Football Club funds.

During this time the Football Club went from strength to strength, the first team gained promotion to the First Division of the Border League, the second team was promoted to the Halstead and District Premier Division. In 1985/6 the club won the Suffolk Primary Cup, and in 1997/8 it won the Suffolk Junior Cup defeating Bungay in the final. At the same time the youth team grew up and became members of the Sudbury Sunday League. Several members of the youth team became regular members of the first team.

Unfortunately the demographics of the area, and lack of competitive sport in schools, meant there was a big gap with no chance to continue the youth team. Luckily with a new generation of footballers this gap is being filled by Glemsford Gladiators.

Over the years the nature of village football has changed. Greater mobility has encouraged a greater catchment area, but also different work patterns and type of resident have made this essential. Since the war, Cavendish never has been a one village club. Now this is even truer. A further change has been drinking and driving, which has greatly curtailed bar takings which were a great source of income.

Soon after winning the Junior Cup things started to go wrong. First the Sunday team folded for lack of players. Then almost all of the young men who had graduated from youth football to club football, good club players and club members such as Paul Mizen, Alistair Younger, Nick Butcher etc, moved away from the village in pursuit of their careers. Just as damaging, a number of strong club members who for years had provided those essential behind the scenes personnel were also lost to the club, Terry Forrester, Ivor Golding, Fred Chowles to name but a few. Dean Brace resigned as first team manager because the job was so demanding that it interfered with his career. All this happened at the end of the 1998/9 season. This impacted on the players, many of whom drifted to other clubs.

During the 1999/2000 season the club was forced to step down from both the Border and Halstead leagues incurring heavy fines. Things looked desperate. Without the football club it was likely that the cricket club would not be able to afford the very fine but expensive facility. The only solution was to look for a club with which to amalgamate. Several clubs were approached but they all called off when they found out the full cost of the operation. The best prospect was the Glemsford team which wanted to progress but could not do so with the limited but cheap facilities at Glemsford. Once again cost was a problem but the Cavendish Parish Council agreed to help finance the changeover for three years. Since then the Parish Council have also helped the sports club with costs to decorate the pavilion.

Up to now this all seems to be a success. Glemsford Cavendish United now has teams in the third divisions of the Border League, the Halstead League and the Sudbury Sunday League. Results this year suggest promotion could be in the offing.

As far as it is possible to trace back, **Cavendish Bowls Club** has existed since a group of gentlemen used to play bowls on the lawn of the Manse in the 1930's and on the park, where there was also a tennis club.

Around 1947 a small bowls green of three rinks was laid on the Bull meadow which at that time was owned by Mr and Mrs Cant who were the landlord and landlady of the Bull.

Some of the prime movers at the time were Fred Kemp, Charlie Creane, Ted Creane, Tom Doe, Herbert Mortlock, Harry Cutmore, Noel Clark, Snowy Brown and Stan Bullock. The club joined the Steeple Bumpstead League in 1953 and have been members ever since.

Several years ago the club were able to purchase the Bull meadow and the club started to expand and grow. It was decided to develop a six rink full size green.

At the Bowls Club   *Denise Davies*

Thanks to their secretary, Ken Doyle, the club were able to obtain a lottery grant with the rest of the money being raised in various ways. The Bowls Club now has one of the best playing surfaces and greens in the district.

The club has a membership of about sixty and runs five teams, three in the Bumpstead League, one in the North Essex Federation and one in the Sudbury Triples League. It continues to grow and flourish.

In June 2001 the club lost one of its longstanding members with the death of Dick Ling who lived in one of the Hyde Park Corner Cottages by the village green. Dick played regularly for the club and also helped to coach members of the West Suffolk Visually Handicapped Bowls Club who played on the green at Cavendish.

Many **other sporting activities** have taken place over the years. In 1924 the Bull used to have a quoits club and they used to play on the meadow to the east of the Sue Ryder Home where there are now bungalows. The Darts Club was based at the George and they used to hold home and away matches. Tennis was a popular pastime. There used to be a court behind the Grey's. This was before the allotments were there and before Grey's Close was built. In later years a group of people would play in a far corner of the Sports Ground behind the Memorial Hall. A badminton club meets weekly in the Memorial Hall from September to May and the game is played informally at other times.

POSTSCRIPT

Cavendish people are proud of their heritage. As Dick Comyn the postmaster once said;

'Whatever the future holds for our children and all of us who live in the village it is hoped that future generations succeed in perpetuating the unique charm that is Cavendish.'

BIBLIOGRAPHY

Barnard, J.D - *Bygone Cavendish* - 1951
Bishop, A.C, Wooley, A.R, Hamilton, W.R - *Minerals Rocks & Fossils* - Phillips 1999
Brimble, L.J.F - *Trees of Britain* - MacMillan & Co Ltd 1948
Copinger, W.A - *Manors of Suffolk* - T. Fisher Unwin 1905
Dymond, D & Martin, E (Eds) - *An Historical Atlas of Suffolk* - 3rd Edition 1999
Kemp, W - *Kemps Nine Daies Wonder* - new edition Larks Press 1997
Perkins, Benjamin - *Trees* - Savitri Books Ltd 1984

INDEX

Allotments, 150, 151
Ambrose family, 23, 68
Ambrose, Basil, 11, 23, 27, 30, 54, 138, 150
Ambrose, Thomas Edward, 23
Ambrose, Tom, 11, 23, 27, 46, 54, 69, 79, 149, 152, 153, 154, 155
Any Lengths Hair Care, 68
Annual Fair, 142, 143
Ark Farm, 40

Blacklands Farm, 23, 31, 35, 40, 56, 113, 114 133, 155
Blacklands Hall, 19, 21, 34, 46, 47, 56, 74, 80, 81, 89, 109, 144, 151, 152
Blacksmith, 36, 37, 38, 69, 114, 129, 132, 133, 134
Blue Monk Cottage, 79
Bowls Club, 157, 158
Brownies, 93, 145
Bull, The, 134, 135, 148, 157, 158

Cavendish Care, 28, 29, 149
Cavendish family, 1, 9, 11, 15, 16, 63, 97, 98
Cavendish Hall, 9, 40, 47, 52, 64, 67, 77
Cavendish Ladies, 145, 147
Cavendish Mill, 49, 66, 127, 134
Cavendish Players, 141, 142
Chinnerys, 54, 72, 121
Chippins, 55, 78
Charities/Trusts
- Ambrose, 25, 30
- Care, 28, 29
- Endowed school trust, 29
- Finbow-Ambrose, 25, 30
- George Savage, 23, 26, 27, 72

Church
- bells, 11, 98
- cemetery, 61, 100, 135
- choir, 100
- churchyard, 54, 58, 60, 100
- clock, 11, 99
- organ, 100
- rectories, 103

Cinema, 23, 70, 85, 130
Colt family, 12, 16, 17, 18
Colts Hall, 1, 8, 11, 12, 13, 17, 18, 31, 36, 39, 40, 67, 112, 125, 150
Community Council, 93, 151, 152
Cricket Club, 22, 23, 152, 153, 154, 155, 156, 157
Cubs, 145

Debenhams, 55, 70, 71
Domesday Survey, 1, 6, 7, 8, 13, 66, 106
Dower House, The, 55, 74
Dramatic Society, 22, 80, 140, 141
Ducks Hall, 40, 47

Fir Tree Farm, 39
Fir Trees, The, 65, 126
First Millennium, 4
Five Bells, The, 98, 138, 139
Flora and Fauna
- hedges, 46, 47, 56, 59
- river, 49, 50, 51, 52, 55
- village, 52, 54, 55, 56
- woodland, 47, 48
Flower Guild (St Mary's), 151
Flower Show, 21, 142, 149, 150
Forget-me-not Club, 149
Football Club, 154, 155, 156, 157
Footpaths Association, 151

Garrett family, 19, 22, 89
Garrett, Henrietta, 20, 21, 77, 92, 104, 136
Garrett, Joseph Stammers, 19, 20, 22, 73, 74, 75, 76, 79, 81, 104, 112, 125, 131, 136
Garrett, Samuel John, 19, 21, 22, 42, 136, 152
George, The, 108, 113, 136, 137, 147, 152, 159
Grammar School, 71, 84, 130
Grape Vine, The, 69, 83, 92, 129
Green End, 67, 68, 138
Greys, The, 68
Guides, 145
Gymkhana, 144

Hale, Joe, 38, 68, 126, 127, 138, 141
History Society, 152
Home deliveries, 125

INDEX

Horticultural society, 79, 149, 150
Houghton Hall, 8, 11, 13, 14, 31, 32, 33, 34, 39, 113, 142
Hyde Park Corner Cottages, 23, 27, 29, 54, 71, 114, 158

Kanavadis (Kanavadisc, Kanvdisc, Kavanadisc), 7, 8
Kimson, 40

Iona, 75, 76

Law and Order, 112
Layfield, 66, 67, 107, 150
Literary and Debating Society, 80, 140
Lych gate, 101, 102

Maltings, The, 19, 21, 75, 76, 125, 130, 132, 136
Manor Cottages, 69, 129
Melford House, 71
Melcott House (and Peacocks), 77, 78, 122
Memories of Old Cavendish (Joe Hale), 126
Memorial Hall, 20, 22, 24, 25, 30, 57, 75, 79, 89, 103, 112, 122, 133, 141, 144, 147, 150, 151, 159
Middle Cottage, 72, 73
Mother's Union, 145
Moone House, 65, 66
Moors Farm, 40

Nether Hall, 8, 9 10, 11, 23, 54, 67, 75, 76, 94, 99, 114, 153
Nether Hall Farm, 40

Old Grammar School, The, 69, 83, 85, 130
Old Post Office, The, 76, 150
Overhall Manor, 8, 9, 10, 11, 66, 75, 76, 103, 107, 108, 142, 150

Parish Council, 21, 23, 24, 30, 54, 143, 151
Peacocks (& Melcott House), 77, 78, 122
Playgroup, 79, 92, 144, 145
Post Office, 75, 134, 150
Public Services
- electricity, 72, 113, 115
- fire, 38, 72, 113
- health, 106, 107, 108, 109, 110
- water, 110, 114, 115, 118, 119

Rabbit Clearance Society, 144

Railway, 19, 20, 50, 58, 69, 86, 116, 117,118, 119, 120, 127, 132
Railway Arms, The, 132, 133
Red House, The, 66
Red Cross, 148, 149
Reminiscences, 38, 94, 95
Road – A1092, 5, 109, 111, 120, 122, 123
Robbs Farm, 40
Royal British Legion, 147, 148

Schooling
- British School, The, 20, 22, 23, 80, 83, 87, 89, 90, 91, 133, 138
- Grammar School, The, 23, 69, 71, 83, 84, 94
- National School, The, 83, 85, 86, 87, 88, 89, 91, 94, 101, 111, 138
- Private Schools, 69, 83, 92, 129, 131
- School (today), 82, 83, 85, 92, 144

Scotts Farm, 23, 35, 39, 40
Scout troop, 145
South Suffolk Show, 144
Stage coach services, 77, 116
Station House, 79, 80
St Mary's Church, 56, 96, 97, 100, 101, 147
Sue Ryder Home, 20, 50, 73, 100, 103, 130, 139, 158
Sunday school, 79, 83, 103, 104

Terrace, The, 75
Tokens, 124, 125
Tumbleweed, 72, 73

United Reformed Church, 20, 27, 73, 75, 79, 89, 104, 105, 122, 132, 145

Virginia House, 68

Wales End Farm, 23, 34, 35, 40, 112, 134
Wales Farm, 23, 40
War Memorial, 84, 101, 148
Weather, 42, 43, 44, 45, 47, 127
Western House, 21, 77, 83, 92
White horse, The, 134, 135
Women's Bright Hour, 105, 145
Women's Institute, 22, 79, 80, 145, 146, 147
Women's Voluntary Service, 148

Yew Tree House, 64
Youth Club, 145